Tales from the
Bark Side

My Journey from
Wayward Stray
to Top Dog

Heidi Ganahl

D1416337

Heidi Inc.
Boulder, Colorado

Published by
Heidi Inc.
Boulder, CO 80302
www.heidi-inc.com

Publisher's Cataloging-in-Publication Data
Ganahl, Heidi.

Tales from the bark side : my journey from wayward stray to top dog
/ Heidi Ganahl. – Boulder, CO : Heidi Inc., 2009.

    p. ; cm.

    ISBN13: 978-0-9842530-0-5

    1. Ganahl, Heidi. 2. Businesswomen--United States--Biography.
    3. Success. I. Title.

    HC102.5.G36 G36 2009

    384.555092—dc22   2009937688

Project coordination by Jenkins Group, Inc.
www.BookPublishing.com

FIRST EDITION

Cover layout by David Haight
Interior layout by Brooke Camfield

Printed in the United States of America
13   12   11   10   09 • 5   4   3   2   1

Dedication

This book is dedicated to all the furry friends I've met along my journey who have helped me redefine the way people care for their pets in North America! From the first few dogs that came to play at camp, to the twenty-six "Greekies" we brought from the other side of the world, the dogs have always been my primary focus. They have helped me to spread the message that with animals, there are no boundaries. The licks and nudges have kept me motivated to keep moving when things got "ruff."

Contents

Acknowledgments   ix

Introduction   xi

PART I: FROM WAYWARD STRAY TO TOP DOG

CHAPTER 1   All-American Girl   3

CHAPTER 2   Tragedy Strikes   11

CHAPTER 3   Searching for an Ordinary World   13

CHAPTER 4   The Battle Is On   17

CHAPTER 5   A Doggone Great Business Is Born   19

CHAPTER 6   Sniffing Out Greener Pastures   23

CHAPTER 7   Homeward Bound: Finding My Way   25

PART II: BECOMING YOUR OWN TOP DOG

CHAPTER 8   Where Do You Want to Go?   31

CHAPTER 9   Find Your Passion   47

CHAPTER 10   Sniff Out Your Idea   51

CHAPTER 11 Dig Up Some Bones   61

CHAPTER 12 Build Your Pack   67

PART III: JUST DOGGONE DO IT!

CHAPTER 13 Feel the Fur and Do It Anyway   81

CHAPTER 14 Signs You're on the Doggone Wrong Trail   101

CHAPTER 15 Specific Challenges of Being a Woman Entrepreneur   109

CHAPTER 16 Don't Forget to Stop and Sniff along the Way   121

CHAPTER 17 Best in Show . . . and in the Dog House   129

CHAPTER 18 Growing Your Business   137

CHAPTER 19 Focus on the Ball   151

CHAPTER 20 Conclusion: Happy Tails with a Happy Ending   163

About the Author   167

Acknowledgments

I wish to extend my profound gratitude to my family, my friends and my dogs who have helped me persevere through fifteen years of struggle in creating a new life for myself. A special "woof" to Mick, Winnie and Orie—the three pups who got me up out of bed every day with a wet-nosed nudge when things were at their worst.

I thank all of my franchisees who took a leap of faith in joining a young growing brand that had, and has, huge aspirations of changing the dog world!

My sincere appreciation to all of the wonderful mentors I've had along the way in the franchise world, the business community, and in the pet industry.

Finally, big hugs to my husband, Jason, my daughter, Tori, and my mom and dad for supporting my efforts to tell my story and continue to live every day to the fullest!

Introduction

I don't believe we necessarily "control our own destiny." I believe our destiny is created by how we respond to life's events.

Through personal and professional tragedies, beginning with the loss of my beloved, young husband, to losing a $1 million insurance settlement, I have triumphed over extraordinary adversity. By turning my lifelong passion for dogs into the largest dog-care franchise in the world, creating a related charitable foundation, and raising a wonderful daughter as a single mom, I feel I have accomplished great success. Through these experiences, I have gleaned personal wisdom and business acumen, which I am happy to share with those who are searching for fulfillment, wishing to find strength to face life's personal and professional challenges, or those needing inspiration to start their dream, or expand their company.

Intertwined throughout my personal story, I will detail the lessons learned from my years of building Camp Bow Wow, from the first camp which opened in Denver in 2000, to a $35 million business with more than 200 franchisees in thirty-eight states and Canada. I will also show the value of giving back as you grow your business. My inspiration? The dogs! This book will illustrate how accomplishment and success can be fraught with many bumps along the way to becoming a top dog. Each step in the journey is necessary to learn, become inspired and gain confidence to reach your ultimate goal.

I gain strength by telling my own story of struggle. Although I understand my specific tribulations are not relevant to many entrepreneurs, I hope my words of perseverance spark inspiration, and my perspective on business fuels the hunger of hopeful business owners and leaders everywhere. This book is designed for my fellow venture seekers, with some sections pertaining to being a woman and/ or a mother in a business world. Even though I stand proud in being a resource for these amazing women, the themes of adversity and balance are applicable to all walks of life and all entrepreneurs.

Charles Darwin said, "It is not the strongest of the species that survive, nor the most intelligent, but the one most responsive to change." From my experiences, change is what it's all about. Life was not meant to be stagnant or easy—it was meant to be challenging and full of experiences to learn from. The paths you choose make you the person you are—so grab change with a feeling of zest and excitement! Fear of change will paralyze you, while welcoming change will allow you to evolve and keep life interesting!

I hope this story of my journey will inspire all of you would-be entrepreneurs and leaders to kick away the fears that are holding you back and finally make the leap you have been dreaming of. Tragedy, loss, misfortune and overwhelming responsibility have led to my tenacity and perseverance. These are traits I have cultivated to overcome the fear that stalls so many from achieving both personal strength and greatness as a leader and entrepreneur. *Tales from the Bark Side* is the story of how I did just that. If I can do it, then, doggone it, you can do it, too!

Carpe Diem! Seize the day!

Part I

FROM WAYWARD STRAY TO TOP DOG

CHAPTER 1

All-American Girl

My journey starts with a smooth ride through adolescence and young adulthood. Born in Southern California in the heart of the sixties, I was born to a Newport Beach surfer, who loved to drag race, and a blond beauty who came from a wealthy family with high expectations for her. The two met at a beach party and quickly fell in love—much to the chagrin of my mom's parents. They expected her to marry a sophisticated gentleman from an established family. My dad was a fun-loving, handsome and adventuresome young man from a family struggling to raise four boys on little income. They didn't have much money, but they had a lot of heart.

My parents quickly married and I arrived soon after. My dad worked three jobs to make sure my mom could stay home to care for me. My brother (who is seven years younger than me) and I were always a first priority. Regardless of the money struggles, we always had what we needed to flourish. I had a wonderful childhood and was surrounded by grandparents, cousins, aunts and uncles, and several families that became our lifelong friends. Dawn Marie was born a short three months before me and lived in the apartment next door with her parents, and my folks' close friends, Diane and Donald. She would become like a sister to me and help me through my darkest moments later in life.

My father launched a career in sales and was successful in making his mark with several companies. My father's parents, Betty and Harv, or Ma and Da as I nicknamed them, lived nearby and were a huge part of my life. My grandmother would inspire me with her tremendous heart and unconditional love for her family.

My grandfather was a huge influence on me, too; he told me to reach for the stars and to use every bit of my smarts to do great things. All of my family had strong morals and values that they worked to instill in my brother and me. I grew to be a lot like my father—outgoing, creative, optimistic and energetic—but I also had a splash of my mom's conservative, determined resolve. Combined, these traits helped create my entrepreneurial, driven spirit.

I changed schools often throughout elementary school, due to the number of new schools constantly being built in Southern California. I believe this helped me learn to meet new friends quickly and become pretty outgoing. My parents and extended family were strong believers in working hard at education, and they encouraged me to strive for good grades and to get involved in school activities. My dog Daisy, a Benji look-alike that I received for my third birthday, was also a big part of my life as well.

At the age of twelve, my dad had a job opportunity in Colorado. My parents decided it would be best to raise us outside of California in a more rural area, so we packed up and moved to Monument, Colorado—a town of about 7,000 people north of Colorado Springs. Three other families from Southern California that we were very close with (Dawn Marie's family included) joined us in the move. I was devastated at first, not wanting to leave my friends in California, and most of all, not wanting to move away from my grandparents, whom I adored. I remember refusing to speak, or even to look out the window at the Rocky Mountains the whole drive to Colorado.

Our new house was fabulous. It sat next to streams, forests, a fishing pond, and the beautiful mountains. It took me a couple of months to warm up to the new environment, but once I did, I truly loved being outdoors (although I really missed the beach). We spent a lot of time that summer with the three other families who had moved with us from Southern California.

My first day of seventh grade at my new school, I wore my pink checkerboard Vans shoes (a staple in Southern California at the time) and a Mr. Zogs surfing shirt. I was quickly labeled a transplant due to my different dress and slight Valley Girl twang. One of several boys who had fun at my expense was a twin cutie who would become one of my best friends in the coming years, and eventually my husband and the father of my daughter. I also was surrounded by some of my best future girlfriends in that room that day—Tina, Molly and Crickett.

I eventually lost the California drawl, and the Vans, and fit in quite well with the small-town group. I had a wonderful time in high school—cheerleading, playing for the varsity soccer team, heading up student council, and being nominated for prom and homecoming courts. I was focused on good grades, but I still had time to socialize and get into my share of trouble. I was truly the "All-American Girl."

From the moment I was born, this "All-American Girl" was extremely strong-willed. I knew what I wanted and I knew how to get it. My exuberant nature worried my parents, wondering how I would be able to cope when the inevitable happened. However, I also found a way to make lemons into lemonade. From childhood troubles in cheerleading to adult heartaches of losing my love, I stared adversity in the face and pushed harder. I wanted to be liked, but more than anything, I was sensitive to the feelings of others. A social girl, I had a take-charge nature that was as natural to me as breathing. My teachers would praise me as a leader that the other kids looked up to and wanted to be around; if someone needed something, Heidi was the one to ask. I valued the importance of extra-curricular activities, participated in soccer, cheerleading, and was on the student council.

My go–getter attitude gained momentum from childhood into adulthood. I dreamed of being a successful advertising executive in Los Angeles or New York, and I worked toward getting a scholarship to a top school to make sure I had the qualifications to do so. I scored a full ride to Southern Methodist University in Dallas, and I prepared to leave my "big fish in a little pond" world behind.

Before I left for SMU, I met Steve and fell into a serious relationship with him. I did leave as planned for SMU, while he remained at the University of Southern Colorado. But I missed him—and my hometown friends—tremendously once I started school in Texas. I had been so excited to go away to college and get away from Monument, and here I was homesick and missing my friends to the point that I was having a hard time adjusting.

After Christmas break, I tried out sorority rush to my mom's delight (I was a Delta Gamma legacy). I joined a sorority with my roommate and another close friend Melanie. The Delta Gamma girls made me feel like I was home at SMU. At the end of the year, my grade point average was a 2.8, thanks to a struggle with economics that year. It was short of the 3.0 I needed to keep my scholarship. Ironically enough, though, after being so homesick, I now wanted to stay. I had grown to love it, but couldn't stay, due to the loss of my scholarship. I decided I would transfer to Pepperdine University in California. They still had a partial scholarship waiting for me from the previous year. Unfortunately, my dad was laid off that summer, so instead of Pepperdine, I lived with my grandparents, went to Cal State Fullerton, and worked two full-time jobs while going to school to pay the bills.

At the end of my sophomore year, Steve was having a hard time starting his career as a journalist, so he decided to join the Army to cover the summer Olympics in Korea. I decided I missed Colorado and the "real" college atmosphere, as Cal State was a commuter school. I headed back to Colorado to attend the University of Colorado at Boulder, which turned out to be a fantastic decision. I graduated from the University of Colorado with a degree in business administration and marketing. I was always very creative, but my business drive permeated my life.

During my time at CU Boulder, I was busy working at the University Business Research Division, which prepared me for a business environment by teaching me how to write business plans and research business metrics. Being in a sorority, I held the role of director of public relations for the Panhellenic Association.

I was also active in my community and involved with the philanthropic efforts that come with being a sorority member. I also coached a twelve-year-old girls' club soccer team for several years during and after college, and mentored several of the girls who were struggling. I later obtained my Masters in Healthcare Administration from the University of Denver.

On the personal side, I had a fabulous time at CU, making lots of new friends, rejoining my sorority, and reconnecting with a friend from high school, Deanna, who would become a lifelong best friend.

Steve came home the Christmas break of my senior year and suggested we should plan to marry upon my graduation and his completion of the Army assignment. Two weeks after he left, however, I got my first reality smack from life. I got a visit from my folks. They said that Steve's mom had called to say Steve had eloped that weekend with a girl he had met in the Army. Four years together and not even a call to tell me himself. I was devastated and very angry. As I look back now, I realize that it was absolutely the best thing for me, but it hurt like hell at the time.

Despite my struggles, I firmly believe that college is vital. It is the essential steppingstone to your career. It prepares and teaches you how to be accountable, how to network, research, live on your own, and manage your expenses. Now a successful business owner, I am a strong advocate for a full education. I'm on the advisory board at the University of Colorado for the Leeds School of Business. With Metro State College, I am on the board for the Center of Innovation, a new entrepreneur-based program. Finally, I'm on the Denver Venture School advisory board, a charter high school that teaches low-income kids the steps needed to get into college and eventually to start a business. It also teaches the preparation needed to become an entrepreneur and how to own your own business.

I'm all about education for *everyone*. I think it's the key to improving our world. Showing my support for the fundamentals is important. My parents sacrificed an incredible amount, sometimes working two jobs, to make sure my brother and I could go to college. There was never a question of *if* we would go—it was assumed. Not only does my involvement on various educational boards stress the importance of a college education, it also enforces my mission to give back.

On the other hand, professional experience is an integral component in starting and running a successful business. I am a firm believer in exposing yourself to as many work opportunities as you can, starting at an early age. Dating all the way back to my teen years, every job experience has contributed something to my work ethic and business acumen. I worked at Dairy Queen all throughout high school to pay for my own car insurance. Not only did I learn responsibility, I also learned how to juggle a packed schedule.

After graduating from CU, I decided to move to Southern California and go after my dream of hitting it big in advertising. I landed a job in San Diego at a well-respected agency. At the same time, my sorority sister Jill landed a job there for a public relations firm. It was the start of a wonderful, close friendship, and the start of a two-year party for us. Jill and I were both very outgoing, so we met tons of people and entrenched ourselves in the San Diego social scene. We found ourselves riding in limos, attending yacht parties, and mingling with stars and the elite young crowd of San Diego. It was a blast, but I burned out financially and emotionally after a couple of years.

I moved back to Colorado in early 1990 and answered an ad for a pharmaceutical sales position. My friend Deanna had stayed in Colorado, so we quickly reconnected and had a great time being single in Denver that spring.

A romantic at heart, I had grown up with starry-eyed expectations of meeting the perfect man, having a very successful career, and, of course, the requisite 2.5 kids. I met my first love at a dance club in downtown Denver in June of that year. My friend Aline and I were mending our wounded egos from recent break ups with some short-term boyfriends, so we took our misery out for a night on the town. Bion and his friend Rich asked the two of us to dance and the rest is wedding bell history. Aline married Rich, and I married Bion!

We spent that night having the time of our lives dancing and laughing with our future husbands. Bion was adorable, charming, sweet and fun—too good to be true. We became the best of friends, and any insecurities I had about being with such an incredible guy melted away as he loved me for what I was. We were both very ambitious and both of us were "dreamers." Bion was what I would consider an old soul. He had a bit of a difficult childhood, but it never showed—he was confident, super-friendly, and was always focused on the positive.

It was the person he was inside that left me both inspired and weak in the knees. He had the biggest heart, and there was not a pretentious or mean bone in his body. Shrewd and ambitious, he put himself through college without the help of his folks. He also didn't have any fear, a trait that still guides many of my decisions today, and helps support me when things get rocky.

Above all else, he shared my love of dogs. He was the type that would stop and pet every dog along the street wherever we went. We both gravitated toward our canine friends, and we couldn't wait to get a house so we could have several. His mom told me stories of him following dogs home to make sure they made it home OK in his neighborhood.

Shortly after Bion and I moved in together, we rescued Taso, who was the first addition to our family. He was an adorable, fluffy version of a fox, who taught me my first lesson about grief; he died only a couple of years after joining our family of urlichia, a rare tick disease. He was only three. We were heartbroken, but it was an insight into tragedy, and it helped prepare me for the tremendous loss I was on the verge of experiencing. His heroic attempt to beat a horrible, quick death inspired me and made me proud to have had him for even a brief time.

Bion and I began building a life together full of happiness and with a limitless sense of hope for the future. We were two highly motivated, energetic twenty-somethings with entrepreneurial spirits and an abundant supply of energy. He was busy finishing college at CU Denver and working full-time with my dad, who had recently started a janitorial supply company that ended up being quite successful.

That was 1992, and Bion and I were constantly dealing with the lack of places to leave our two pups, Mick and Winnie. I was frustrated that I couldn't find an appropriate location that met my standards, and I felt guilty about relying on our family and friends to watch the dogs whenever we needed help. The idea for Camp Bow Wow came from neighboring inspiration. We used to check out a day care for dogs called "Doggie Day Camp," and we enjoyed just watching the dogs play. It was located right next to my dad's business, and was one of the first doggie daycares in the country.

With this expanding trend in pet care and the inspiration of "Doggie Day Camp," Bion and I started to brainstorm an alternative to the bleak conditions of the traditional kennel environment. We asked the owner of the doggie daycare if she was interested in selling it to me or franchising. She said, "No, there are plenty of dogs. Start your own company." So I adopted some of the services she offered and developed some of my own.

"Doggie Day Camp" was a good start to an idea, but it had some problems. We liked the daycare concept, but she just had a big, ugly warehouse with all forty dogs milling around. We created the idea of a camp for dogs and the "all day play" theme so that dogs wouldn't be stuck in a kennel all day and had freedom to play with their friends. We even considered having one of those cutting-edge web sites! Keep in mind this was only 1993!

Seven years later, when I decided to make the Camp Bow Wow plan a realization, there was not much I needed to alter. To my delight, the services Camp Bow Wow provided were highly accepted and clients immediately began dropping off their dogs to be cared for. The response was wonderful—many looked at their pups as members of the family and felt secure there was finally a place for them to be cared for. The next step was obvious: to expand into the option of overnight boarding. This addition proved successful because clients didn't have to rely on leaving their dogs in a chain link crate or box for days at a time if they had the engagement of travel or work. Also, my inventive concept of a safe and fun place for dogs helped relieve the guilt not just for dog owners but for dog-lovers who always wanted a pup but couldn't because of their busy schedule. Camp Bow Wow finally made it feasible for busy people to add a new furry friend to their family.

Camp Bow Wow distinguished itself right of the bat. First, the camp-like ambience plays a large part in our brand and signature. Each camp offers indoor and outdoor play areas that range in size between 4,000 to 12,000 square feet. The different sections cater to the freedom of your pup being able to wag his tail and stretch his legs without the constraint of a leash. Camp is all about fun—we use the tag line "Your dog should have more fun than you on your vacation!" We knew we also had to appeal to the owners' likes, too, thus the upscale log cabin feel of the lobbies and marketing materials. Being from Colorado, we thought it was a perfect fit for our market. Then it evolved into a place "where a dog can be a dog," and the slogan coincided with our camp concept. I did not want a fufu spa place for dogs, I wanted a rough and tumble, have-fun-at-all-costs kind of place. Some dog care facilities give manicures, massages, have TVs, luxury suites, etc. We have indoor and outdoor play yards with slides and ropes and campfire treats each night (Kong's with peanut butter inside), and lots of freedom to run and chase and wrestle. They can bark to their heart's glee! At night, we play classical music to soothe the pooches to sleep.

Being a young couple from middle-class families, Bion and I had lacked the resources to start the business on our own. Based on our own experiences looking for a place to care for our own furry friends, Mick and Winnie, we knew the market was ripe for an alternative to the old kennels and vets for boarding dogs. Unfortunately, the plan was shelved indefinitely when tragedy struck just twenty-six months after we wed.

CHAPTER 2

Tragedy Strikes

One of my husband's many wonderful traits was his thirst for adventure. He was spontaneous, fearless, and loved extreme sports. Bion's twenty-fifth birthday was approaching, and my family was starting to plan the perfect gift for him. One day, my dad ran into a good friend, named Cliff, who was a seasoned United Airlines pilot. On the side, he had a 1943 Stearman biplane. This was an open cockpit biplane that he took to air shows and used to perform stunts. Cliff proposed the idea of my dad coming along for a ride. Instead, my father thought this would be the perfect surprise birthday present for Bion and asked if he could come as well. My dad and Bion were very close friends, and my dad loved him like a son. Two days after Bion's birthday, on May 14, he left early to go meet my parents at their home in Monument.

Bion and I had just moved into our new house in Parker and we were ready to build that house into a home. That day, there was a community garage sale and I decided to participate, since we had lots of extra odds and ends to clear out. I kissed my husband and waved goodbye. Contrasting the dark cloud that would befall, it was a beautiful Colorado spring day. I remember how blue the sky was.

My mom and dad escorted an excited, but curious, Bion to meet Cliff at the Meadowlake Airport in Colorado Springs. Bion was thrilled when he realized the surprise. Bion would go first, and my father planned on taking a ride when Bion was finished.

The ride started off great; they did all the crazy stunts that Cliff had performed at the air shows and decided to finish with a fly-by over my folks. My parents were watching from down below on a stretch of road near the airport. They were in contact with Cliff through a radio. Cliff buzzed in to my dad and told him to get the cameras out and prepare for the fly-over.

The plane started downward from about 2,000 feet high, and suddenly dove into the ground about 75 yards from my parents. My dad ran to the plane and found both of them dead upon impact. Chaos ensued. My parents were devastated and in shock from just witnessing the unforeseen death of their beloved son-in-law. My parents were forced to stay at the site and deal with the commotion, so they called my little brother, who was back from college and at their home in Monument for the weekend. He drove the thirty minutes to Parker where he broke the news to me at the garage sale.

I saw him appear in my mom's car, and the look on his face was unrecognizable. He blurted out that there had been a crash—and that Bion was gone. I immediately went into shock as I dropped to the ground. My world was turned over with a wave of panic. I could not breathe and I could not think. The pain was palpable.

Patrick drove me back to Monument, where my parents had returned to their house. It was horrifying. It was surreal, I was so numb that I felt I was not in my own body. To top off my pain, I had to make the call to both of Bion's parents to tell them about the tragedy. They were shocked and angry and, months later, harshly blamed my family for buying him the gift. Friends and family from all over the country came to support us and share in our devastation. The nights were filled with periods of hyperventilation, waking up in a sweat, and lots of sobbing. The days were filled with stories of Bion, sharing our grief, and dealing with the media that had a deep interest in the story. The paperwork, decisions about the funeral, the phone ringing non-stop, and the constant flow of flowers and visitors was overwhelming. I desperately wanted my old life back.

The death of my husband and Cliff, a long-time, involved member of the community, became very public and the press was everywhere. The community rallied around my family and gave us wonderful support. But the attention was also suffocating.

I had no clue how much that day would truly change my life, my priorities, my family, and my future.

CHAPTER 3

Searching for an Ordinary World

The coming days became more and more arduous, as I was overcome with misery. Completely trapped in my own punishing inertia, the thought alone of moving on was formidable and downright impossible. Bion's untimely death had a paralyzing effect on me. I lost sight of all the hope that gave me the drive to make something of my life. All the energy and spirit I once had was channeled into all the wrong directions.

My dogs, Mick and Winnie, were instrumental in helping me through this time. I felt so alone and I didn't want to burn out my friends and family by bringing them down all the time. This was just my own personal reservation, because on the contrary, my family and friends were wonderful and extremely supportive. My close friends Dawn and Deanna sat with me time and time again while I sobbed uncontrollably, heartbroken. My younger brother, Patrick, stayed with me during my time of need to help out and comfort me. I spent a lot of time at my grandparent's house in California, and at my aunt and uncle's house in Florida. I found relief through reading and listening to music. It felt good to get away from the intensity of my life back home in Colorado, where everyone knew what had happened to me. The phone would ring constantly and people would stop by trying to help, but all I wanted to do was to hang out with my dogs and figure out how to survive.

Before I could push through my grief, I had to travel a very rough road. When Bion's death left me with a $1 million insurance settlement, just three months after the crash, I was stricken by what to do with my financial windfall. I felt extremely guilty about the money, like I should not be rewarded for losing the love of my life. It's called Sudden Wealth Syndrome, and it's very common to have a lot of guilt over receiving money through a settlement. Most folks (approximately 75 percent) who receive large settlements or lottery winnings lose it all within three years.

The fall after Bion died, I felt this constant panic that I would never again have a "normal" life. I had a plethora of new titles, and I did not feel comfortable with any of them. I was now known as "the widow," "the girl whose husband died in the crash," or "the girl who got rich off the plane crash settlement." I just wanted my all-American life back—the life where I was once so happy, married, living in suburbia with my dogs and adorable husband. I craved filling my void with a happy life, complete with kids and a great career.

My good friend Cindy convinced me to go to my ten-year high school reunion. Seeing my best friends from high school was the emotional filler I needed. I felt this return to being just the "girl from Monument," a title I embraced immediately. These were people who knew me before the bad stuff happened in my life, before the pity. I was back to being recognized just as "normal Heidi." At the reunion, my old guy friend (remember the boy in seventh grade who made fun of me?) explained he was living in Glenwood Springs, Colorado. I had just rented a house in Aspen for a month to get away from my life back home.

Kyle (not his real name to protect Tori) had just gotten out of rehab for getting two DUI's and, unbeknownst to me at the time, he had severe addiction problems. He seemed to be on the mend, and I was mending too, so we found a likeness in each other. He made me laugh for the first time in months, and was able to cover my terrible loneliness, just a bit.

Kyle turned into a band-aid for the desperate loneliness I felt, and we fell into a dating relationship. It was during this time that the reality of the crash started to set in and I experienced raw, unrelenting grief. My doctor put me on an anti-anxiety drug for the panic attacks and the severe depression I was sinking into. What he didn't tell me was that this new medication would prevent my birth control pills from being effective. I got pregnant, and was shocked and scared to death. I cared about Kyle, but I was still madly in love with Bion. I didn't think there was any way I could handle this emotionally, and I really didn't want to be tied to him indefinitely with his addiction problems. It was starting to become very evident that he did not have his act together regarding the drugs and alcohol.

My counselor helped me work through the options, and we decided I should move forward with the pregnancy, regardless of how ill-equipped I felt toward being a caregiver. I couldn't even take care of myself! However, the psychological effects of *another* loss in my life would be detrimental and hard to recover from. He and my parents were very supportive, but I received some horrible reactions from other people about me getting pregnant within a year of Bion's death. One family member told me that I had "stabbed my grandmother (the one I adored) in the heart," and that I was headed straight to hell. Others would look at me with horror like, "What have you done?" or "Obviously you didn't love Bion as much as you claimed, if you could do this." I also didn't want people thinking I loved Bion any less because I had been hanging out with this friend and was dealing with a pregnancy. I felt guilty and ashamed.

I did, however, feel this strange calm that if this baby had found its way to me through birth control, severe depression and the fog I was living in, there might be a damn good reason she was to come into my life.

Kyle wanted to marry right away, but I just couldn't, since I knew I was still in love with Bion, and was not close enough to recovery that I could focus on a new relationship. Also, I was learning more and more about his deep addiction issues. We did stay together and moved into a home back in Monument near my folks and his family. This also meant that we were in the hotbed of gossip in our small town—the same town that had been so supportive when Bion died.

Our relationship was very rocky. I had a horrible time dealing with the ups and downs of living with an alcoholic while I was still on an emotional roller coaster myself. I was dealing with Bion's death, the sudden windfall of money, and my pregnancy. In addition, I had started Nursery Works, a catalog company for baby supplies that was a ton of work. Kyle's alcoholism and drug use flared up often, but I looked at it with the "I-can-fix-it" attitude that most people who don't understand addiction do.

On the flip side, getting pregnant was a blessing in disguise because it made me stop drinking and feeling sorry for myself. If the baby hadn't come into my life, I fear I would have resigned myself to the alcohol, drugs and depression that were starting to get a deeper grip on me. I just didn't care much about anything. Suicide wasn't an option, as I loved my dogs and family too much to submit them to more pain and agony. So I lived in purgatory—living each day, but in a fog of just surviving, not thriving. I tell people to this day that it comes down to waking up every day and deciding if you are going to live that day as if you are choosing to live, or choosing to die. Once the reality of the pregnancy set in, I started to care for myself again and embraced the role of sustaining a healthy growing baby.

Tori was born a beautiful, happy baby girl, and I was filled to the brim with love for her. Her father got clean for her first year and I figured it was time to give us a chance as a family. I married him to give our baby girl the stability she deserved. The grief over my lost love was still evident with every breath I took, but I yearned for a normal life—whatever that meant.

I found, to my displeasure, however, that a life with Kyle would be more detrimental than "normal." We had a beautiful wedding about the time of Tori's first birthday, but on our honeymoon, he disappeared for three days in Maui on a drinking binge. Things went downhill from there. I tried everything from intensive counseling to pushing him into another rehab visit. We had very different ideas of commitment and marriage, and there seemed to be no middle ground we could find. I was slowly learning another hard lesson about the evils of addiction and the inability of anyone to change an addict but themselves. My "fix it" personality didn't do squat.

At the same time that I was desperately trying to make my marriage work, my business Nursery Works took a turn for the worse. We had tried a new marketing technique that failed miserably and basically put the business under, along with about $200,000 of my settlement from the crash. With the money I was spending on supporting our family (Kyle contributed very little of his $8/hour salary to our expenses, since I had "all this money."), loaning money to friends in need, and putting my faith in financial advisors who made bad decisions, I was feeling horribly guilty about blowing a good chunk of the settlement. After being told by attorneys and advisors that I could live forever on the settlement, I felt like a complete idiot.

CHAPTER 4

The Battle Is On

Kyle's addiction problems had led to a tumultuous existence. When he started punching holes in walls, I finally decided it was time to get out. At first, he agreed that this would be best, and we agreed on visitation with Tori.

However, a week after we separated, he got his fourth DUI in five years. He was arrested, but let out on bail and proceeded to show up for his scheduled visit with Tori, who was then two. He wanted to drive her to Colorado Springs, and I said absolutely not; driving with her was out of the question. His court hearing for his charges was the next week, and it was inevitable that his driver's license would be revoked. I gave him the alternative of supervised visits at the house.

His mother was a constant enabler of all of her four kids, and rushed in to save her son from her deluded perception that I was "controlling" him. She then proceeded to hire a tenacious father's rights attorney to battle my perceived "control" of him. Since that was not enough to hurt me, the attorney started to go after my $1 million settlement from Bion. He claimed the prenuptial agreement was invalid because it was signed too close to the wedding day.

The following months, and years, would be some of the most stressful times in my life. He and his mom were battling me tooth and nail to get whatever money they could, as well as wanting equal custody of Tori. His alcohol and drug problem was not enough to keep the courts from denying his "parental rights," or denying his mom from her "grandparent's rights." I could write an entire book on the injustice in the family courts, and the lack of good decision-making around the children. It's disappointing that a parent's or grandparent's rights trump the safety and well-being of a child.

They simply worked the system—his mom obtaining the visitation rights, then openly handing Tori off to her son, who was a mess. I was horrified, and did everything I could to protect Tori from her dad's drinking and driving, and having our sweet little girl around his addict buddies and non-stop girlfriends. I asked the courts to institute drug testing, I hired a Special Advocate to represent Tori, I provided evidence over and over of his and his mom's system to cheat the courts by using her as the front for her son's custody, all to no avail.

The courts are overwhelmed, and unless it's a dire immediate situation, they do nothing. I started saying no to his mother and to him, regardless of what the court said, which ensured that the battle would keep escalating. I didn't care as long as Tori was safe. I always allowed her dad and his family to come visit Tori at our home, at McDonald's, or at a local park, even when things were at their worst. But they seemed to care more about "winning" the battle, rather than spending time with Tori, since they rarely visited.

After the first few years of the ugly, expensive custody battle, I was in my darkest hours. My fight ate away my settlement from the plane crash, and I squandered the rest on unreturned loans to various friends, a series of bad investments, and the failure of two start-up businesses that I founded. I continually focused on being a good mom and shielding Tori from the ugliness of the battle. I dug deep within to the values and ethics I grew up with and decided to fight for what was right for my daughter (and to use the settlement to do that if I needed to). I would earn the money back the old fashioned way with hard work and commitment.

When most people would be sane enough to walk away from the dream of owning their own business during all this, I stood firm and held hope that I would get a successful business launched some day. I felt this tenacity and determination that I would not let Bion die in vain, and that all the dreams and aspirations he and I had would still come to fruition. It also became a priority to set a great example for my young daughter.

The battle went on for six onerous years, cost over $400,000, and left my family and me emotionally devastated. For all the excruciating pain that Bion's death brought, this matched it in a much different way.

CHAPTER 5

A Doggone Great Business Is Born

During this intense time, I took a second shot at being an entrepreneur. I launched a consulting firm, The Maginot Group. My goal was to earn my Certified Financial Planner designation and help others deal with the crazy emotional side, as well as the practical financial side, of inheriting "sudden wealth."

When I received the $1 million settlement, I was faced with an onslaught of advisers, brokers and lawyers vying for my business. I was also besieged by friends and acquaintances who either needed to borrow money or wanted me to invest in their business ventures. I would ultimately hire and fire two financial planners, who earned me a return of less than five percent on my money while the market was enjoying double-digit yearly gains, before deciding to go it alone in the spring of 1997.

The consulting firm did not sell securities or manage money, but helped clients evaluate their financial health and goals, estate-planning needs and options for hiring professional help, such as whether to use a stockbroker or a financial planner. It also provided them with an overview of stocks, bonds and other investment options, and helped formulate a plan of action. In many cases, it also helped clients interview and hire advisers. I provided clients with references to seasoned planners, estate-planning lawyers, accountants and grief counselors.

It was rewarding work to be able to sit down and understand where these people were coming from, as there is a good sense of freedom because you have all this money and all these choices, but it can be overwhelming. At the same time, I became frustrated, as I watched my clients make the same mistakes I had made, regardless of how much I warned them. I also felt guilty "making money" off these folks, so I often didn't charge them, or gave them a much-reduced fee. I didn't want to be one of those considered to be taking advantage of their situation—the exact thing I was trying to prevent.

With the stress of the custody battle, the emotionally draining work I had been doing with The Maginot Group, and the life of being a single mom, I was at the end of my rope. My brother and the rest of my family sensed this. In the fall of 2000, my brother came to me and asked me to consider dusting off the old Camp Bow Wow business plan, and get busy doing what my heart wanted to do from day one—build a business around dogs!

I had $83,000 tied up in a variable annuity from my settlement, and had just taken a part-time pharmaceutical sales job to make ends meet. My brother offered to do the day-to-day operations of the business if I would take on the marketing and business side, in addition to my pharmaceutical job. I put aside any fear I had of losing the last of the money and called a broker to help us find a site. We did just that within a couple of weeks—an old Veterans of Foreign Wars hall near downtown Denver. It was in bad shape, but with the help of my mom, dad, brother and some good friends, we painted and repaired ourselves into a frenzy and made it happen! We opened Camp Bow Wow in December of 2000 and had our first furry customers the day after our grand opening. I worked my sales job and, at the same time, marketed the new business like crazy, all the while running back and forth to do my mom stuff as well. A lot of people who knew me thought I was nuts for trying another business, especially one that was as far-fetched as a doggy day care.

The business grew quickly, and my brother and I managed to work through some initial rough patches of running the business together. We had some incredible times in that first year or two growing the camp. Our first big interview with the *Rocky Mountain News* was on a busy weekday at the camp. I was running late, so my brother showed the reporter around and happened to yell at some pups, "Hey, no humping!" Well guess what the headline of our first big story was? It worked out great, as it generated a lot of fun buzz.

We spent a lot of time doing charity-focused events and sponsoring fundraisers for local dog charities at the camp. In the first year, we took advantage of my brother's involvement in a band and held two music events—"Punk for Pets" and "Music for Mutts." We had a "Fido Formal" on Valentine's Day and held a big "Howloween Party" in October.

We experienced some not-so-fun things running the business, as well. Some of these included: employees not showing up in the morning to open, our innovative web cams constantly being down, our first outbreak of kennel cough, a crazy owner of another dog day care smearing us in the press to try and put us out of business, veterinarians who thought our concept of letting dogs play together was nuts, and going through six types of different floor finishes to see what would hold up. It was a ton of work, but completely and utterly satisfying and fun.

About a year into opening Camp Bow Wow, one of our clients came to us and suggested we open a second location at her dad's veterinary clinic in northwest Denver. I had still not made any money back from the business and was working non-stop on the first camp while raising Tori as a single mom. I thought to myself that I should be conservative and go slow with opening a second camp. Then the entrepreneurial "Heck, yeah!" part of me blurted out, "Of course!"

My family helped me build out the Broomfield, Colorado, location, and I stopped working my pharmaceutical job to focus on the second camp. I used credit cards and a small line of home equity credit to launch the camp. I remember sitting on the floor laying tile in the middle of the night before the big grand opening, thinking, "What the heck did I do?" My credit cards were maxed, I had no savings left and the first camp was breaking even, but not making a profit. Then, all of a sudden, a calm came over me and I knew—I just knew—that things would be OK.

Many people ask me if I had a vision to grow Camp Bow Wow into a franchise leader. I knew it would be something big, something special, but I did not have a specific plan to franchise. Bion and I set out to change the way people care for their dogs when they can't be with them. We wanted to provide people with a fun, safe and happy alternative to leaving them home alone or in a dark, lonely kennel. That was our only goal, and I think Bion would agree that we are now achieving that goal with every new camper that joins us around the country!

CHAPTER 6

Sniffing Out Greener Pastures

During the first three years when I was launching Camp Bow Wow, I was still dealing with the custody battle. I constantly received nasty letters and legal accusations from my ex-husband's attorney about my parenting skills, my focus on my new business, and my lack of respect for my daughter's relationship with her father. They went after my parents and my friends with accusations as well. Every time I got a letter, I had to pour the emotional and financial resources into defending myself. They wanted alimony, child support and full custody at one point! It was surreal—I kept thinking, "The courts will back me at some point; they will not let this happen. It's so clearly unfair and not right."

Finally, on the recommendation of my fourth attorney (I kept getting better and more expensive attorneys), I waged a final court battle to move based on my potential marriage to my current boyfriend, and my company's need for a West Coast location. I filed the paperwork, waited the nine months for the court date, escaped their grip on my life, and packed up Tori to move to Los Angeles in 2004.

I had already started franchising Camp Bow Wow at this point, but the business was still in its infancy. I was sure I could manage it from Los Angeles.

I left my long-time friend and business partner, who had a background in franchise operations with a large franchisor, in charge of operations in Colorado, and I focused on sales and development from LA. It wasn't easy juggling travel, Tori, the dogs and a growing start-up, but the relief I felt from being away from the hell of the custody situation made it bearable. I was able to spend time with my grandmother, my aunts, uncles and cousins, which made for a fun family time.

We didn't hear much from my ex-husband or his family after we moved, other than a very occasional phone call from them to Tori. They had fought so hard for rights to Tori for so long, and now that the battle was over, it seemed their interest was over as well. It broke my heart for Tori.

As much as I disliked all of them and was horrified by their treatment of Tori and me, I still recognized that this was her blood—her father and his family—and she needed a relationship with them. I did my best throughout the battle, and during the time on the West Coast, to not talk badly of them and to talk about the good attributes she inherited from her father. I also kept her in counseling to help support her efforts to understand the situation. She was a healthy, happy child who seemed fairly oblivious to the short deal life had handed her in the father department. Luckily, my dad had stepped in to take on that role as much as he could.

Tori and I loved Manhattan Beach. It was beautiful, fun, and the perfect size for a mom and young daughter to explore. It felt as though we were on an adventure, and we thoroughly enjoyed living near the beach and our family. I traveled a lot to manage the business, but I always had a friend or family member to help me with Tori. We missed my parents and our friends back in Colorado, but living near the beach meant we got lots of visits from all of them!

CHAPTER 7

Homeward Bound: Finding My Way

Camp Bow Wow was continuing to flourish, as franchise sales slowly grew and new camps opened on a consistent basis. During one day in the summer of 2005, the phone started ringing off the hook unexpectedly. America Online had featured Camp Bow Wow as one of the next great franchises on the cover of its web site! AOL had picked up the story off of the Internet from a small article *Business Week* online did on women in franchising. The phones and e-mails went crazy for weeks, and we scrambled to handle the 2,000-plus leads we received from that one day!

Things started ramping quickly, and as I focused on sales and marketing, I trusted that my friend and business partner in Colorado was handling the operations side of the business. She also handled the books. She and I had known each other since she dated (and later married) Bion's best friend. They had divorced, but she and I had remained friends. When I started franchising, she was working for a large franchisor in Denver, so it seemed like a great fit to have her help me out. I gave her a percentage of the franchise start-up company as an incentive, since I couldn't pay her much, and we dug in to build the company together.

That fall, I started paying more attention to the books, and noticed some questionable charges on the company credit card and withdrawals from the bank account. My heart sank when I realized that she had been taking money from the company. My good friend of fifteen years, whom I trusted completely, was embezzling. I spoke with my attorney before I said anything, and was told to change the locks, fire her immediately and file charges. The emotional devastation of having my friend take advantage of me hurt far more than the thousands of dollars she took. I was floored.

I was able to win back her shares in the company based on the charges, but it didn't do much to heal my emotional hurt. I flew to Colorado, took control of the remainder of the business, and fired her operations director. I was suddenly the only one left operating the entire franchise company, and doing it from 1,000 miles away in California as a single mom.

It wasn't easy, but I pulled together some new people to help me, and did my best to support the franchisees and my daughter while I figured all of it out. I was able to juggle living in LA with running the company until late August 2006, when I made the decision to move back to Colorado and set up our corporate headquarters in Boulder.

As of the printing of this book, we've sold more than 200 franchises in North America, have launched a new in-home pet care, training and grooming franchise, called Home Buddies, and are growing our non-profit division—The Bow Wow Buddies Foundation. We've been featured on *The Big Idea*, in *Success* magazine as one of the Top 10 Franchises They Love, annually we are included in the Franchise 500 of *Entrepreneur* magazine, and I recently won a Stevie Award for Top Entrepreneur. Camp Bow Wow has recently been named to the Inc 500, has been named one of the top companies in Colorado, one of the 88 Fastest Growing Franchises in the country by *Entrepreneur* magazine, one of the 50 Fastest Growing Women-Led Companies by the Women's President's Organization, and we have been awarded a "World Class Franchise" designation by FranSurvey.

We have big plans for the future, including opening over 1,000 camps in North America, 1,000 Home Buddies franchises, and building our non-profit to one of the key forces in the pet industry to help with pet overpopulation, humane treatment, and curing canine cancer.

I look back and realize my current focus, lack of failure, minimal fear, and determination to make the world a better place, stems a great deal from the horrifying loss of Bion, the brutal custody battle that ensued and the various challenges I met starting Camp Bow Wow with little money and little time. My start as an all-American girl, with little adversity and lots to be thankful for, gave me the basis to persevere through the horrifying, crazy events of the last fifteen years, and end up more balanced, more sure of myself and more faithful than I ever thought possible.

My life has come full circle in some aspects. Meeting my husband Jason a couple years ago and the success of Camp Bow Wow has helped bring back that sense of being the "All-American Girl" once again. Jason's optimistic attitude and easy-going personality has been a great balance to my almost panicked "live life fully before it all goes away in an instant" way of being. I've begun to trust again that the rug won't be pulled out from under me at any moment, although part of me knows it's possible and that I'll be able to handle whatever is thrown my way.

And after years and years of feeling like an outcast, dealing with labels like "widow," "single mom," "business flop," "the girl who blew a million bucks," I'm now a wife, mother, successful business owner and just a "plain old girl" in most aspects.

As I tell my story to groups around the country I emphasize how important it is to embrace your own "story" and realize that the "All-American" lifestyle isn't about having a perfect, smooth experience in life, it's about adapting and creating a wonderful life out of the struggles, joys and challenges thrown your way.

Part II

BECOMING YOUR OWN TOP DOG

CHAPTER 8

Where Do You Want to Go?

"Will you tell me please which way I ought to go from here?" said Alice.

"That depends a good deal on where you want to get to," the cat responded.

"I don't care much where."

"Then it doesn't matter which way you go."

—*Alice in Wonderland*, by Lewis Carroll

As you've heard in my story, passion can indeed pay the bills. Passion will build the value of your business. Passion will wake you up every day with a hop in your step and a glimmer in your eye.

If you feel chained to the desk, and each day is as mundane as the next, you, like many Americans, need to be at the head of the pack, instead of dragging at the end. Clasp your hands together, interlock your fingers, and notice which thumb is placed on top. Now re-clasp your hands to place the opposite thumb on top. It feels unnatural doesn't it? That forced feeling is synonymous to a born entrepreneur who is placed in the constraints of the corporate world.

We see the world differently: Opportunity, instead of security, and long-term results, as opposed to short-term gain. Excitement, independence, and creative freedom are some of the advantages of being your own boss.

Starting a business is not free of risk, but it is not as unobtainable or far-fetched as many believe. According to the IFA Educational Foundation:

- 55 percent of all Americans want to be their own boss.
- 37 percent of all households are involved in small business.
- 70 percent of all high school students want to start a business.
- One out of every twenty-five adults is currently starting a business.

The current recession has brought the inner entrepreneur out of many unemployed workers. Plenty are burned-out looking for work at yet another corporation, so instead of sending in their resume, they're channeling their inner-inventor and composing business plans. In fact, if these entrepreneurs succeed, the outcome could turn the ailing economy around, because small companies are big employers. In 2008, according to the Bureau of Labor Statistics, 3.8 million small companies that had less than ten workers employed 12.4 million people, or in other words eleven percent of the private sector work force.

However, even in a flourishing economy, the odds are not good for an entrepreneur to succeed. According to the U.S. Small Business Administration, over 50 percent of small businesses fail in the first year and 95 percent fail within the first five years. Drawing from these statistics, we can safely say starting a business is survival of the fittest.

Regardless of our current economic state, if you have been bitten by the entrepreneurial bug and are thinking about starting your dream business, you need to consider what type of business you are prepared to start. You can either be an independent business owner, or a franchisee.

When it comes to jumping into the entrepreneurial pool, some people dip their big toe in, while others dive in head-first. You must determine where you are in your life and how much you are willing to give to a start-up business. On the flip side, you need to calculate how much you are willing to lose. What route to take is ultimately determined by how you answer one question:

"How comfortable are you with risk?"

There are many qualities to being a successful entrepreneur, one of them being that you have to be willing to take risks. Starting a business is based on risks—you need to be able to deal with the consequences. Failure and problems will be inevitable. From bad investments to two unsuccessful start-up companies, I have a lot of failure under my belt. But quitting was not my contingency plan, I kept trying until I made it and that meant going back to where my passion was.

If you prefer consistency, you might be looking for a lower-risk business alternative. An example of a low-risk business might be starting a web-based company, while maintaining another job to pay the bills. Or, if you have the cash to start a company, but still want a more consistent approach, a franchise or major chain might be the best alternative for you.

Franchise Agreement

Franchisor	Franchisee
Owns trademark or trade name	⟶ Uses trademark or trade name
Provides support: • Financing (sometimes) • Advertising and marketing • Training	⟶ Expands business with franchisor's support
Receives fees	⟵ Pays fees

85 percent of franchised businesses are still operating after five years. Most franchisors (the people who sell franchise rights) screen prospective franchisees for business knowledge and experience. Some franchisors also offer extensive training programs, ongoing management assistance, and a systematic, rather than a trial-and-error approach to running a business. For a fee, most franchisors increase the probability that the business will be successful. While success is not guaranteed, franchisees' track record for success is higher than first-time, independent business start-ups. Most franchisees succeed. Most independent businesses started by first-timers do not. Consider this:

- The franchise industry accounts for 40 percent of all retail sales in the United States, and one out of every twelve businesses is a franchise.

- The average net income for a single-unit franchise is $76,000, and $142,000 for a multi-unit franchise.
- Franchises will generate more than $1 trillion in sales this year.
- While franchises only account for 8 percent of all service business, they claim over 40 percent of all service-related revenue.
- Franchises currently employ more than 21 million Americans.
- More than 300 different types of industries and businesses are now franchising, and a new franchise opens every five minutes, accounting for 35 percent of all retail goods and services sold.
- From the U.S. Department of Commerce, less than 5 percent of franchise outlets fail annually.

By contrast, according to statistics derived from the U.S. Small Business Administration, during a ten-year period, over 60 percent of non-franchised businesses shut down within the first six years, due to failure, bankruptcy or retirement.

If you have that drive to run a company, but not the drive to start one, buying a franchise might be a smart decision. You already have a proven success model, and you already have a support system. When an individual wants to purchase a franchise from Camp Bow Wow, they are required to follow a strict franchise agreement. We provide them with the support and tools to make the business successful. Our group is consistently improving and evolving the business to make sure it stays successful. You just need to select the right franchise and make sure you'll be working for something you are passionate about. While the economy continues to nosedive around the country, the franchise industry trend will be to grow—not slow down. Historically, franchises experience renewed interest during periods of economic upheaval, and the current downturn is proving no different.

If you think a franchise might be right for you, take time to do your home-work. First find out what franchises are available. Read directories, such as:

- *The Franchise Opportunities Guide*
- *The Executives' Guide to Franchise Opportunities*
- *Bond's Franchise Guide*
- *The Franchise Annual*
- *Franchise Handbook*
- *How Much Can I Make?*

Read articles and ads in business publications:

- *Inc.*: www.inc.com
- *Entrepreneur*: www.entrepreneurmag.com
- *Franchise Times*: www.franchisetimes.com
- *Franchising World*: www.franchise.org
- *Franchise Update*: www.franchise-update.com
- *The Wall Street Journal*: www.wsj.com
- *USA Today*: www.usatoday.com
- *The New York Times*: www.nytimes.com

If you swing for the fences and shoot for the stars, then entrepreneurship is probably in your heart.

Before you start your business, though, you need to assess yourself as an entrepreneur to identify your strengths and weaknesses. There are numerous resources available to help you determine whether you have the right personality and skill mix to be an entrepreneur. One of my favorites is Michael E. Gerber's book, *The E-Myth Revisited.*

ENTREPRENEURIAL SELF-ASSESSMENT:

FROM THE IFA EDUCATIONAL FOUNDATION *An Introduction To Franchising 33*

Starting a successful business takes a tremendous amount of energy and certain personal characteristics. Read each of the characteristics below and circle the number that most accurately describes your entrepreneurial potential on a scale of one to ten. (1 is low, 10 is high)

Characteristic Description Your Tendency (low to high)

Motivation, drive, energy to succeed 1 2 3 4 5 6 7 8 9 10

Enthusiasm, excited involvement 1 2 3 4 5 6 7 8 9 10

Risk-taker, willing to take chances 1 2 3 4 5 6 7 8 9 10

continues ▶

Confidence, sure of your own abilities 1 2 3 4 5 6 7 8 9 10

Competitiveness, wanting to win 1 2 3 4 5 6 7 8 9 10

Perseverance, refusal to quit a task 1 2 3 4 5 6 7 8 9 10

Creativity, imaginative thinking 1 2 3 4 5 6 7 8 9 10

Organization, keeping things in order 1 2 3 4 5 6 7 8 9 10

Vision/leadership, knowing where you want to be 1 2 3 4 5 6 7 8 9 10

Persuasiveness, ability to convince others 1 2 3 4 5 6 7 8 9 10

Honesty, truthfulness 1 2 3 4 5 6 7 8 9 10

Adaptability, can handle new situations 1 2 3 4 5 6 7 8 9 10

Understanding, can sense people's feelings 1 2 3 4 5 6 7 8 9 10

Self-discipline, sticking to a plan or schedule 1 2 3 4 5 6 7 8 9 10

Independence, belief in oneself 1 2 3 4 5 6 7 8 9 10

Purposefulness, doing things for a reason 1 2 3 4 5 6 7 8 9 10

Goal-oriented, work steadfastly toward a goal 1 2 3 4 5 6 7 8 9 10

Problem-solver, think of solutions to problems 1 2 3 4 5 6 7 8 9 10

Drive, desire to work hard 1 2 3 4 5 6 7 8 9 10

Optimism, positive attitude 1 2 3 4 5 6 7 8 9 10

Date _____ Total Score _____

Your score is an indication of the extent to which you possess personal characteristics similar to those of successful entrepreneurs.

The Probability of Your Entrepreneurial Success

A Score of 160-200

You possess very strong entrepreneurial characteristics. You will probably find entrepreneurship a very desirable, exciting and fulfilling way of life.

A Score of 120-159

You are mildly entrepreneurial. You may find entrepreneurship desirable and stimulating, but may have to develop your entrepreneurial abilities through training.

A Score of 120 and Below

You will probably find entrepreneurship undesirable and difficult. You will probably be more successful working for someone else, although you can still develop your entrepreneurial abilities. So, if you are determined to start your own business, don't give up!

This quiz is a rough exercise based on common entrepreneurial abilities. There is no real test to see if you have it or not. You need to take into account where you are in your life and if you can really put forth the effort to pursue your dreams. To really know yourself will help define your passion—the root of a successful running business.

You must ask yourself these three questions when starting or expanding your business:

"Where have you been?"

"Where are you now?"

"Where do you want to go?"

If you are aimless in your approach, you will never really be able to propel your business to success. Without focus, we are poor leaders.

If you are going to start a business, be prepared to focus on your objectives. But first, let's focus on where you've been.

Focusing on the Fundamentals: Education vs. Experience

Grooming yourself to become a top dog, or an "alpha dog," starts when you are young and full of self-confidence. It does not require being stubborn or selfish—it simply necessitates being demanding of yourself, taking risks in school or in your job, to go above and beyond your required responsibilities, being loyal and committed, and always following through. It starts with your first job out of school and making the most of any experience you can.

When reflecting back on your education and life experience, ask yourself:

- What did you like to do? (Interest and hobbies)
- What did you know how to do? (Experience)
- What did you do well? (Special skills and talents)

Reflecting on your past reveals useful information for your future. I want you to take out a pencil and record the following:

1. Acknowledge your successes from past or current jobs. Write these down and evaluate them. What are the patterns? Pinpoint your strengths and accentuate them; identify your weaknesses and eliminate them.
2. Figure out what working environment you have previously favored, and how you can bring that ambience to your company.
3. Think of past co-workers and colleagues. Who complemented your working style? If you were lacking certain traits, what did they bring to the table to balance out the team?

What we gather from different corporate work experiences can influence our professional credibility. I've been in the "corporate world" when I worked in the pharmaceutical industry, and I learned both good and bad lessons. In fact, many people at Camp Bow Wow have lived the corporate life. They understand some of the positive things it teaches, and know how to shape our organization's culture accordingly.

It's rare to love every little thing about your job, and common to dislike most of it. For me, this is the difference between having a boss, and being my own boss. Now I wake up every day ecstatic to go to work. But this was not always the case. In pharmaceuticals, I found each day as mundane as the previous. Entrepreneurship? Love it! Corporate America? Not so much. This doesn't mean I haven't learned many invaluable lessons from my experiences. The lessons learned in a corporate world can be directly applicable to your self-started business.

Helpful Things I Learned in Corporate America

1. **Self-Discipline:** No entrepreneur can be successful without discipline. In the process of turning an idea into a business, it takes a level of control and self-regulation to go through the mundane prep-work. No one enjoys hours of bookkeeping, but you have to really put the time and effort into making every last piece fit. There's no one to keep on your back if the work isn't finished, no superior to answer to. You're your own boss, remember! You don't always see the short-term consequences, so to accomplish the not-so-fun tasks, you need to have discipline.

2. **Composure:** Let's address the inevitable—problems do happen. You know there are going to be failures, so it's up to you to take charge. A good entrepreneur manages to stay calm amidst a crisis. As the leader, it's up to you to put out the flames, but also to keep your cool when the heat is on. Freaking out or blowing up will only intensify the problem.

3. **Patience:** The ultimate virtue. How many times have you had to wait, and wait, and wait, for something to get accomplished in the corporate world? Progress is slow in corporations, but it is also slow in a start-up business. Limited cash-flow, limited human resources, or outside vendors can often get in the way of getting something done quickly in your own business. Have faith, and remember that all things good are worth the wait. Make good use out of the waiting periods by checking, and checking again that the process is going well, and the end product will be a success.

4. **Focus:** Unfortunately, potential and existing customers always have a tight hand on the microscope. So if you never sweat the small stuff,

you might want to start. A small slip-up might be your biggest expense. In large corporations, losing one or two—or even three—customers won't always impact your business. But as entrepreneurs, we have to look at the big picture *and* pay attention to the little things. Attention to detail will keep you ahead of your competition. Once your business grows, you can hire someone strictly to worry about the details, but until that point, hang in there. It may seem tedious and unnecessary at times, but the benefits will outweigh the costs. Always keep your eye on the ball!

5. **Responsibility:** Always hold yourself accountable; no one is going to hold your hand at your job like they do in a corporate environment. You are your own best resource and, most days, if you are not involved in your start-up, it doesn't get done.

6. **Professionalism:** You are representing your company, brand, or service, so conduct yourself according to your own professional standards. From the way you think to the way you act and dress, you are forced to uphold a level of professionalism, both in the corporate world and in running your own business.

7. **Balance:** It's not uncommon to get caught up in your work to the point of obsession. With so much pressure, so many little things to be accountable for, you can easily push day-to-day operations past the average working hours. There's no question you're going to eat, sleep, and breathe your new company, but you can always take it too far. You can keep your company at the well-oiled machine level, without turning into a work robot. The delicate balance of when to hang your hat is only controlled by you. Remember how many elements go into your personal life, and how you can re-calculate your schedule accordingly.

8. **Teamwork:** At any corporation, you are trained to work on a team. Remember when you were interviewed and they gave you the team scenario question? As in, what would you do if one member of the team were doing something wrong? How well do you get along with others? And other questions like that. Companies love these questions, partly because to answer them correctly, you need to have the mind-set of a team player. That doesn't stop when you start your own business. Your team is your lifeline when you are an entrepreneur!

Not So Helpful Things I Learned in Corporate America

1. **"Pawlitics:"** Corporate America and politics go hand in hand—there could not be one without the other. The world is run not only by what you know, but also by whom you know. In the office, your co-workers might be working with a hidden agenda, and you might learn that for yourself. It's a cutthroat world of office politics, with the mindset of every man for himself. However, there's a difference between good and bad politics. Good politics is working with the system for the betterment of the company. In this case, the business objectives are pure and good for the company, such as focusing on satisfied customers, or bringing in new revenue. Bad politics is when someone works the system to better his/her personal situation. Bad politics are all around; I see it daily from little actions to enormous ones. Dealing with such people in corporate America teaches you better hiring and management skills to deal with these situations once you run your own firm. Set the boundaries from day one that negative politics won't be tolerated. Once it starts, it's hard to stop.

2. **Micromanagement:** Encarta Online Dictionary defines the term micromanage as: "attend to small details in management: to control a person or a situation by paying extreme attention to small details." Think Michael Scott from the comedy television show *The Office*— many corporate bosses take this type of management control to a whole new level. If you have to micromanage someone on your team, it's a bad sign. Either there's a lack of trust, or you think they are incapable of doing what needs to be done. Really evaluate if they are the right person for the job. If they are, it's time to set the goals. Meet regularly but not constantly, and give them a chance to prove themselves. In the long run, if that doesn't work, neither will micromanagement.

3. **No Room for Creativity:** It's a constant frustration when employees don't search for creative solutions to problems in the organization. Without creativity, there is no innovation and no potential for positive change. A lot of employees that started in corporations have had their creativity stunted. Working for a start-up requires constant creativity and innovation—let those creative minds you hire loose!

4. **No Efficiency:** Corporate structures have often led to failures in collaboration, communication, and efficiency. Many corporations strive for a more productive workforce, and center on promoting efficiency. Efficiency is great if it's inspired and effective in obtaining a team goal. If it's simply a tool to stay busy, that will absolutely not work in a start-up environment.

5. **Lack of Communication:** By acknowledging the lack of communication in many corporations, we can determine how to effectively run our own companies. Many of you have probably been treated as disposable as paper plates at times. Understand how you felt about that, and how it made you feel hesitant to act like a team player. Since the leader of a business is as strong as the pack behind it, you know to never allow such disproportionate disrespect—it's all about proving you care by communication. Developing a team you can trust sustains a well-oiled working machine.

Traits of Successful Entrepreneurs

To beat the odds, successful start-up owners appear to have three things in common:

First, they are prepared.

Once you find the passion to start a solidified idea, there are a ton of outlets out there to help you organize and fine-tune your approach. You are the driver, but education is the global positioning system (GPS)—guiding you where you need to go.

- Research your tail off and talk to as many people in the industry as you can. The U.S. Small Business Administration is a great resource for any beginning entrepreneur. I took many trips to their office to ask questions, explore info they had and figure out how to correctly start a business. With a branch office located in every state, the SBA can help you with everything from the basics of starting up, to the problems associated with marketing and employees.

- For inspiration in your field, go to trade shows and industry association meetings.
- Join an organization related to your business, or one filled with other budding entrepreneurs.
- Find some mentors, those admirable individuals who are doing what you want to do. Take those leaders out to coffee and pick their brain. I guarantee the lessons you pick up will trump any course you could take.

It was hard for me to network at first; people in the dog business are very protective and less social than those in other industries. There's a reason they're in the dog business—they want to hang out with dogs, not people!

Learning is just as important as leading; you need to be able to absorb lessons and teachings from those who have paved the way before you. Look at each opportunity and individual as a page in your business textbook. *Read, read, read!*

In terms of hands-on activities, seminars, and educational experience: Be a sponge. You need to be teachable. Soak up whatever information you can, and then work through what needs to be filtered out. Don't get bogged down in doing all these things—at some point you just run with it! I think there is a balance that needs to exist for every personality and leader. It certainly doesn't pay to set off on your own without learning from others and considering their advice. But in the end, only you know your true vision.

Second, they often have experience in the area of business they are starting, or a similar type of business.

Do not get involved in a business you know nothing about. You are already taking a risk by starting a business in the first place, so make sure it's something you can stick with. The more you know about your industry, the more protected you'll be. Any work experience dating back to your first job is valuable, and you should expose yourself to as many work-related opportunities as you can. Try to integrate yourself in the field, even if it's part-time or temporary. If not only for the exposure, it's a great networking tool as well.

Third, they know how to market themselves.

Since building a company is about selling your brand to the public, you need to know how to sell yourself and your ideas. You are your company, so learn how to be the CEO of YOU. Learn how to integrate yourself into the community by networking, taking professional development classes, or even starting a blog. My website, www.heidi-inc.com, focuses on my life as a successful female business owner and how my personal trials can be inspiration for others. I write and post my Top Dog Blog on both of my websites – the Heidi Inc. site and the Camp Bow Wow site. It is an extremely useful and effective outlet for keeping the public in the loop with both my personal and professional life.

TOP DOG BLOG

My crazy dog days . . .
May 2nd, 2008
My days start with a lick and a nudge from a big black wet nose Ray Ray, my lab, has an internal alarm clock like the official international time clock! Soon afterwards, my iPhone chirps away with the sounds of iPhone's crickett noises—much to the delight of Scout, my lil' 3 lb Maltese rescue that wakes to that sound each morning and truly believes the lil' critters are hopping around evading him and looking to play!

As my boyfriend kids, from the moment I wake my brain starts with "dogs, dogs, dogs, dogs, breakfast, dogs, dogs, dogs, Tori school, dogs, dogs, dogs, dogs, drive to work, dogs, dogs, dogs, dogs, franchising . . ."

I arrive at the office to find about forty e-mails and ten voicemails— even though I left the office at 6 pm the night before! I try not to work in the early evenings, but spend time with Jason, Tori, Raider and Scout—hiking, making dinner, watching our goofy favorite shows (Should I admit we love American Idol? We flip between that, the basketball playoffs and Fox News in any given hour . . .) or playing games on the Wii. After the rest of the house is fast asleep, I get some time to catch up on e-mails from the day and work on various projects or programs.

The days fly by with meetings and short sessions of return phone calls and e-mails—today my meetings ranged from a quick muffin for breakfast with my in-house counsel to quickly review documents, a meeting of our franchise relations and real estate teams to discuss some new programs to speed the openings of our camps and lower budgets, a quick session to discuss a potential partnership on a new dog movie, a phone call about speakers for our coming annual meeting, a photo shoot for some upcoming press, and finally to wrap the afternoon up, a meeting with our CFO to discuss April camp data. Another 100 or so e-mails flood in throughout the day, and my voicemail fills with calls from various vendors, franchisees, team members . . .

. . . and even with all of these distractions, my thoughts remain, "dogs, dogs, dogs, eat lunch, dogs, dogs, dogs, pick up dry cleaning, dogs, dogs, dogs, create auction package for Tori's school, dogs, dogs, dogs, walk Rotti our Greekie at camp, dogs, dogs, dogs, stop and pick up stuff for dinne . . ."

It's an absolute joy to wake up every day and love what I do. I love that I have a wonderful family-based business that is focused on something I'm so passionate about and allows others to fulfill their dreams of owning a business and caring for our furry friends. It ends with my mind trailing into dreamland back to "dogs, dogs, dogs, snoooooooooooooze . . . . zzzzzzzzzzzzzzz . . . ."

CHAPTER 9

Find Your Passion

For me, my passion was always quite clear—my lifelong love of dogs combined with my love of entrepreneurship. I am certainly a much better person with a dog in my life. I never imagined I would be able to build a business around my love of animals, but I did always know in my heart I would dedicate myself to a career making a difference in the world. Even as a kid, I was always trying to save the spider from being squashed, and I would feed all the stray dogs in the neighborhood.

If you don't have passion in what you do, your job will seem like, well . . . work! Passion is the essence that drives all top business owners to hit their stride every day.

I was validated on this point while guest teaching a class on entrepreneurship at the University of Colorado. It was great fun, telling my journey of how Camp Bow Wow grew into a national brand and the lessons I've learned. I spoke about the challenges of managing teams effectively, protecting our intellectual property, integrating technology into our business, and utilizing cash and precious resources to grow the brand. I told stories of good days—and bad—in the trenches of building a business. I focused on what would help prevent the students from making the mistakes that I and other entrepreneurs have made on the road to success. I anxiously awaited the questions following my presentation about the difficult and complex business challenges I face daily. What came instead were questions about the core of our business—the dogs. It shouldn't have surprised me, but it did. They wanted to know what types of dogs come to camp, how we entertain them, keep them safe, and what the funniest moments at camp had been.

It lightened my heart and reminded me that at the core of any business is passion. It's not complex—it's simple. Do what you love and the success will follow. That's why Camp Bow Wow is a success. All of us on the corporate team, all of our franchisees and all of our staff at the camps have one passion that joins us and makes Camp Bow Wow work—our furry friends.

Before I started Camp Bow Wow, I worked in pharmaceutical sales; not the toughest job in the world, but not the most exciting either. I only worked about seven to eight hours a day and was pretty successful just doing that, but if you're not passionate about what you do, you only do enough to get by. I always spent a few hours a day looking into business ideas; I was a typical entrepreneur stuck in the corporate world.

Let your passion inspire you in life and business. For me, it was my family, and, of course, my dogs. To discuss passion in life and business, look no further than our own furry friends for all the important things we need to know. Our dogs are gifts. They are teachers. They stay by our sides, undisturbed by worry or regret, and show us how to live each moment as it comes. I've learned incredible business and life lessons from my furry friends.

For instance, dogs have goals. Catch the Frisbee, destroy the toy, win the tug of war, and get the longest scratch on the head as possible. They know where they are and where they want to be. For many of us, this is agonizing. Where are we now? What are our goals? Sometime, we have no idea.

Dogs know what they want and they go for it. I've never known a dog that lived life as though it was just a practice run. But we often live our lives like we are going to do it all over again, and the next time around we'll take all the chances. You have to stay connected to your goals—without focus and tenacity, you won't achieve your heart's desires. Our dogs constantly send us gentle examples of this. My dog, for instance, will not quit staring me down until I offer an invitation onto my bed at night. That is the same kind of clarity that we need to pursue our own goals.

Dogs aren't confused about their feelings. They are always pretty clear with how they feel about themselves. If they're satisfied with where they are in life at any one moment, they'll wrestle a toy or take a nap to celebrate. When they find themselves in circumstances that are particularly unappealing, they'll do everything possible—bark, scratch, cry or jump—to stack the deck back in their favor.

Dogs appreciate the simple joys of life—the excitement of heading to the kitchen each morning for a bowl of dry kibble, riding with their heads out the window, or chasing the Kong dog toy down the hall until it bounces off enough furniture to come to a rest on the floor, where it will get the shaking of its life. There's the soft feel of the grass in the backyard, always worthy of a roll or two. There's the glorious word "walk," which to our furry friends, sounds like "Lotto winner." And they are always as grateful as if it were the first time.

Dogs have taught me to appreciate life more fully and assume much less. Their simple and grateful approach to even the smallest gestures reminds me how each moment counts. What do you appreciate in your life? Look at the simple things around you that fill your life with abundance, and that you appreciate. The fact that I can have a dog as a pet and companion means that my life is filled with abundance. If I can recognize that, then every day is a biscuit from the counter, or a Frisbee-throwing session in the sunlight, or a swim in the pond on a hot summer day.

Dogs live, more or less, without the burden of time. I believe that dogs live in fifteen-minute increments. Every fifteen minutes is a brand-new day! If you don't believe me, try and reprimand a dog for a pillow she destroyed twenty minutes ago. She will look guilt-free. Time has already absolved her of responsibility. If you do catch the dog within fifteen minutes, she will forgive herself long before you will.

It's not that dogs can't remember. You can condition their behavior; teach them to sit, lie down, and fetch a Frisbee. It's just that dogs really don't need to remember much. I'm reminded of this during the five-minute walk from our condo to the park. Ray drops his Frisbee at least four times along the way distracted by a smell. I have to remind him to pick it up and to get back on track. Dogs don't have expectations beyond their immediate needs. They're not obsessed with their potential. They're not crippled by regret like the rest of us.

Dogs live totally in the present moment. When you are there, they are happy. When you close the door behind you to leave, they think you are still standing there on the other side of it, and they're happy with the anticipation of your return. Their relationship with time is a good deal different than ours. In many ways, it's a good deal healthier.

T.S. Eliot said, "Time past and time future, what might have been and what has been, point to one end, which is always present." It seems that love can only truly exist in the present moment, and only when we are present in the moment can we truly love. Our pups provide a simpler application. Watch a dog transfixed on a ball waiting for the toss. Watch a dog politely, yet tenaciously, staring at the refrigerator where the leftovers have just been placed. Watch a dog rolling in the soft grass of spring. T.S. Eliot, and a couple of dogs, made sense out of that for me.

Dogs teach us the balance of connection and disconnection. It seems that in our search for a life with meaning there is the paradox that sometimes we let things or relationships mean too much. Whether you are grasping something as fragile as the heart, or gripping an old cherished toy with stuffing exploding from it, sooner or later, you have to let go.

As a human, it's easy to find a purpose and just as easy to discard one. A dog however, never strays from its sense of purpose. Years may pass, but a hound will always dig and a retriever will always fetch. It's what makes them happy. It is important that we, too, find focus for our lives, whether it is our camp, our children, our dogs, a hobby, our faith—or a combination of these things. It is through our focus that we learn the quiet confidence that what we are is enough, that we need not look outside ourselves for validation. I have the companionship of dogs—we all do—to continually remind us of that. Dogs like being dogs, and they like being the dogs they are. That's their sense of purpose. They face the world undaunted, sticking their nose in the air to search for the next adventure—just as you should as a budding entrepreneur!

CHAPTER 10

Sniff Out Your Idea

Questions every entrepreneur must answer after determining his/her passion:

1. What business?
2. Is there a market?
3. Can I afford it?
4. Can I make enough money to make it worthwhile?

1. What Business?

This stage involves an objective assessment of the demand for your product or service. You should be able to verbally explain your idea and purpose in less than thirty seconds—what your company is, what it stands for, what it does, and why you do it. This is your chance to really sell your idea, and a passionate statement makes a believable statement.

When the idea for Camp Bow Wow was born, we created a business plan and my mission was clear for the camp—to help change the way people care for their dogs and offer a fun, safe healthy alternative to kennels. I wanted to see through Bion's and my dream, but mainly my incentive was the need for better dog care across the pet industry. I believed whole-heartedly that our country was ready for a concept like this. I knew there were others who adored their pups and wouldn't stand for leaving them in a kennel or at a vet. I went back to my passion for dogs as a basis for building the business—I was completely focused on making our four-legged friends a main priority. We simply tried to build it around what would make dogs happy, healthy and safe. Also, it can be taxing at times to come home after a hard day's work—and often a lengthy commute—only to find Fido hyper and ready to romp and play for an hour, when all you want to do is kick off your shoes and relax. Occasional trips to your local Camp Bow Wow mean a night or two of rest and relaxation with a dog that is more apt to snuggle than drop a ball at your feet every ten seconds. Others are using Camp Bow Wow as a way to feel better about working all day and having the occasional night out: leave Fido at day camp while you are at work and he will be more than happy to sleep at home while you go out to dinner. It is true that a tired dog is a well-behaved dog. Then there's travel—who wants to feel guilty about leaving their dog when they go on vacation or travel for work? No guilt when you can log on to the Camper Cams and watch your dogs playing, romping and receiving lots of love and attention.

2. Is There a Market?

Who Are Your Potential Customers?

Your business plan will have to present information about your targeted demographic. Their age group, where are they located, their financial status, and their likes and dislikes.

Our franchises are built around DINK's with dogs (double income, no kids, dog owners)—affluent seniors who like to travel and want to leave their dogs behind in a trusting environment, and young professional couples without kids.

Once acquired as sidekicks for kids, animal companions are more popular now with empty nesters, single professionals, and couples who delay having children. What unites these demographic groups is a tendency to have time and resources to spare. With more people working from home or living away from their families, pets also play a bigger role in allaying the isolation of modern life. About 63 percent of U.S. households, or 71 million homes, now own at least one pet, up from 64 million just five years ago. And science is starting to validate all those warm feelings with research that documents the depth of the human-animal bond.

All Successful Businesses Must Either:

- Respond to a trend
- Solve a problem
- Satisfy a need

Respond to a Trend

When compiling your plan, make sure you are not entering a market already crowded with competition. If you have your sights set on a popular avenue, make sure you bring something different that is analogous to the trends today. You must prove, despite the crowded competition, that there is a place for your company, and that it has the essentials necessary to thrive.

Solve a Problem

If you are entering a market that is barely established, it might be harder to sell your pitch, but you should use that void to your advantage. Some of today's gaps may produce tomorrow's success stories. In my case, I based my business on a doggie day camp that was right next door to my dad's business. It was more of a bare-bones operation, with forty or so dogs milling around a big old warehouse. We wanted to offer a safer, more secure environment for our clients' dogs. So we focused on providing a more upscale alternative, with private rooms, supervised playtimes and a lodge-like feel.

Satisfy a Need

Look at your customers and competitors when you formulate your competitive analysis. What unique or original qualities does your company have to offer? What share of the market do you expect to command?

High traffic areas always draw in a crowd. A choice location can also serve as a fantastic opportunity. When I was searching for locations for the camps, I only targeted metropolitan areas. However, I looked at the convenience of the customer and realized that locations close to airports would generate clientele. Also, travelers can drop off their pups on their way out of town and scoop them back up after they land. As a result, we offer a Bark and Park service, so you can leave your car if you choose and catch a ride in our Bark-n-Ride to the airport. It's wise to be continuously thinking of how you can alleviate stresses for your clients.

3. Can I Afford It?

Before you commit yourself to a business, first figure out if you can afford it. Estimate your start-up costs, which include:

- Location design and construction
- Professional fees
- Equipment and fixtures
- Technology
- Opening inventory and supplies
- Insurance
- Pre-opening labor
- Opening advertising and promotion

Estimate how much working capital you will need. This is the money you will need until the business becomes profitable—include your living expenses, if necessary. Working capital includes such things as:

- Salaries
- Insurance
- Utilities
- Advertising
- Rent
- Interest on a loan, if applicable

First, assess your personal finances. Then create a personal balance sheet that lists your assets and liabilities. Become aware of and assess potential financing options (i.e., friends and family, financial institutions, government programs, and funding opportunities). Begin to establish relationships early! Find out what potential bankers or investors need. Determine the factors that contribute to their financing decision.

I started Camp Bow Wow with $83,000 left from my plane crash settlement. I also tapped into credit cards, a small bank line of credit, and occasional short-term loans from my folks or my grandmother. I have essentially bootstrapped the business (which means simply using the money you make from the business to plow back into it for growth capital).

I *do not* recommend this route for the weak at heart. I lived on the edge a lot and made it through some tough spots by getting creative (payment plans with vendors, trading services with vendors, timing growth projects based on our cash availability, and using credit cards when I had to). In the real world, this rarely happens. It's much less risky if you have some financing worked out before you start your business.

When calculating the financial aspect of your venture, always overestimate the amount of cash you are going to need. After your big idea comes along, make sure you have enough money to run the business for at least one year. Then take that number and double it. The number one reason small businesses fail is due to insufficient funding. A lot of people think they can bootstrap anything, and they under-analyze the rough first months of opening a business. It is such a shame when you have to close the doors to your business after only six months due to a lack of funds.

4. Can I Make Enough Money to Make it Worthwhile?

Estimate the profit potential for the business:

- Income
- Expenses
- Profit (income – expenses)

Think about the amount of time and energy it will take to make the business successful. Make a decision as to whether you think you can make enough money to make the entire venture worth your time and energy!

Creating Your "Brand"

The aim of successful branding is to clearly associate the organization, product or service with an image or identity in the mind of the audience. The brand should associate this image with the quality and characteristics of the product or service. A solid brand is a quick way to show and tell the public what an organization represents and what it has to offer.

I have had the opportunity to build a business and define everything, including the culture, based on one thing: bettering animal welfare as far as

I can reach. I attribute the success of my camps to the fact that I have never strayed from my purpose. I focus on the success and the specifics of our brand. I knew from the start I wanted Camp Bow Wow to be huge. I did not want just one camp; I wanted to build a brand that would make a difference in pet care nationwide. It's tricky to produce a brand that sticks out in a consumer's mind above the rest of the competition. For Camp Bow Wow, we distinguished ourselves right off the bat. We took inspiration from my hometown's dog daycare, and we tweaked it to our standards. *This is key to modeling your company off of another: Make it your own.*

You already know that your brand isn't just about your logo, tagline and glossy brochure. But where do you go from there?

1. A Great Brand Lies Inside Your Consumer's Minds

To become a successful brand, you need to first acknowledge and have access to your target audience. Once they realize that your brand has exactly what they need in *performance, price, status, or quality,* you can be in the running in today's competitive market. Granted, your brand needs to shine in any of these four points. Think of your brand as more than a label, a logo, or great marketing. It needs to encompass all of your consumer's needs. It needs to be *true.* You can brag all you want about the superiority of your brand, but if it doesn't hold true to your customers, then you are talking to open air, my friend. Ask yourself these two questions: Will my brand have a share or positive position in the market? Will my brand draw in our customer base and capture their attention? If you answered yes to both, then you most likely understand the importance of a quality brand and a customer-based relationship.

2. A Great Brand Can Go the Distance

In straining economic times, meeting your customers' needs is imperative in keeping your business alive. You need to prove your brand is not a luxury, but a *necessity.* If you can stand out in the clutter of the marketplace, then your brand is in it for the duration. By proving your sustainability, you will have opportunities to transcend into multiple segments, and perhaps worldwide. Embrace the future!

3. A Great Brand Tugs on the Ol' Heartstrings

Emotions drive many, if not all, of our decisions. Basing your brand on quality is key, but gearing it toward human emotions is equally important. I'm not saying you should manipulate your brand to stand for some arbitrary, irrelevant cause to boost sales. Not many people stand around the water cooler discussing the difference between dimpled soles or plastic spikes on a golf shoe. Instead, it's that winning shot that was made, the tense anxiety of the competition, or the way Tiger Woods celebrated his victory that gets attention.

A brand reaches out with that kind of powerful connecting experience. It's an emotional connection point that transcends the product. And transcending the product is the brand. When you see the relief and happiness of a client as they pick up their pup from camp, you know you've filled a void. We provide a way to alleviate guilt for our human clients, by giving dogs back some of the care they give us.

It's about relating your customer to the product. Make sure you state not what your product or service is, but *why* it's so beneficial to your market and to your customer. What does it stand for? Why is it better? If it's a cookie business, is it just like the way Mom makes them? Or for a jewelry company, is the design reminiscent of the Victorian era? Focus on why you are so passionate about your brand, and you will convince your customers that you can meet their needs.

4. A Great Brand Can Truly Be Anything

Camp Bow Wow is all about the deep emotional connection that people are developing with their dogs. We have an opportunity to leverage our top-notch reputation and our devoted customers—both furry and human—to be a great leader in the pet industry and in the retail arena.

It is true that it's easier to brand in certain categories than others. But a common misconception is that you can't make a brand prosper in a narrow category. In fact, by producing your brand, you might have invented an entire new category for someone to copy. Starbucks has not only established itself as a cultural standard for coffee, but a cultural symbol and known entity. With Subway, "eating fresh" became not just a slogan, but also a lifestyle. You have to be distinctly unforgettable and understand that any idea or brand is possible. Camp Bow Wow started as a dream and has now reinvented the standard in pet care.

5. A Great Brand Can Invent or Reinvent

The common denominator you find among brands like Nike, Coca-Cola, and Disney, is that they strive to be the leader in their categories. Nike is the leader in how an athlete strives for their personal best and the overall symbol of sports apparel. With Disney, they hold the position for entertainment for the whole family, upholding certain values and kid-friendly virtues. Coca-Cola backs the quality taste of its product with the tradition and history of a brand we correlate to fun in our lives. All of these brands have paved the way in each of their categories to set standards not only for their competition, but for the way we think about and respond to the values their brands represent.

A great brand raises the bar. It adds a greater sense of purpose to the experience, whether it's the challenge to do your best in sports and fitness, the affirmation that the cup of coffee you're drinking really matters, or the responsibility people feel to choose the best care possible for their furry friends.

6. A Great Brand Knows What Works

Identity, identity, identity. Before you build your brand, you have to know your brand yourself. You cannot get to this level by getting other people's opinions on what *they* think your brand should be. The best way to test a brand is by testing and trials. Go out and talk to the consumers, figure out what they want in a product or service. Research the trends, and find out how you can adapt and modify your idea. Know what you want in your brand, and if you believe in your brand, the brand will speak for itself.

In order to keep it vital and different, you need to be able to constantly change and revitalize your brand. That way you're consistent with quality, but you also keep the customer intrigued by adding new dimensions.

7. A Great Brand Knows What **Not** to Do

A great brand has to know when to grow and when to stay put. If a great brand knows itself, it has to use the knowledge of what does work to know what doesn't work. After you have established your brand, it's smart to continue to revamp, but not to stray too far. Never stray from your mission and what your brand stands for. I stay with pet care, as opposed to other animals segments, because I know that's where my mission and my passion lie—the animals. I have branched into other related products and services because I am continuously looking for ways to meet the clients' and the animals' needs. Our new Home Buddies brand capitalizes on our devotion to pets and our experience in our industry segment. The customers that have trusted their dogs to us for years can now rely on us to care for their other animal friends, as well.

8. A Great Brand Is Always Developing

A brand is a metaphorical story that's evolving all the time. This connects with something very deep. People have always needed to make sense of things at a higher level. We all want to think that we're a piece of something bigger than ourselves. Companies that manifest that sensibility in their employees and consumers invoke something very powerful. The humanization of pets is just a step toward realizing that our furry friends are soulful friends, not "just pets."

9. A Great Brand Is Consistent

Think of a great brand like a promise— a promise that you will continue to deliver a quality service or product. With a promise comes consistency, a quality customers strive to find in a brand. A great brand is like a quality piece of art, it's priceless. It upholds a consistent level of excellence. Sustaining consistency is really quite simple. You just need to focus on your vision and values and stick to it.

Think of what you say and how you say it. If you promise your customers certain advantages, then you need to uphold those throughout. This is why I have implemented rules and standards for all of my franchisees to abide by. If there is one inconsistent camp, the whole brand is affected. That's why hiring, running, and maintaining your pack is so important in keeping your level of excellence at its highest point.

Our brand is everything—it holds the value of Camp Bow Wow. It's what we've all invested in and need to protect at all costs.

10. A Great Brand Is Relevant

The larger idea is for a brand to be relevant. It meets what people want; it performs the way people want it to. In the last couple of decades, there's been a lot of hype about brands. A lot of propositions and promises were made and broken about how brands were positioned, how they performed, and what the company's real values were. Consumers are looking for something that has lasting value. There's a quest for quality, not quantity. It's the difference between PetSmart and Camp Bow Wow. We didn't just use a makeover to pretend to be something different than a "kennel." We changed every aspect of how we care for the dogs. We are relevant, and we are essential to our furry and human clients. We are part of their family. We capitalize on this relationship in order to keep our business growing.

CHAPTER 11

Dig Up Some Bones

Where Exactly Do I Get the Funds to Start?

Sell Assets: If you own things, you can sell them. It's that simple. Jewelry, rugs, pool tables, boats, time-shares, and second properties—the list goes on. Most people's largest assets are their homes and cars.

Borrow Against Insurance Policies: If you want to know where all your money goes, look at your insurance payments. Each month you probably pay for health insurance, life insurance, disability insurance, auto insurance and perhaps homeowner's insurance. Unfortunately, you can only borrow against whole life policies, but most have some cash value after three years. Simply write your agent or insurance company, saying you want a policy loan. Most companies will lend up to 90 percent of the cash value, and your policy stays intact as long as you keep paying the premiums as they come due. However, if you die with a policy loan outstanding, the benefits might be diminished, although that varies by policy. But the good news is that loans against your insurance policy are fairly reasonable, since the rates charged are tied to the key money-market rate.

Borrow Against Your Investments: If you're starting your business part-time while keeping your full-time job, a potentially stable investment is borrowing against your employer's 401(k) retirement plan. It's common for such plans to let you borrow a percentage of your money that doesn't exceed $50,000.

The interest rate is usually about 6 percent, with a specified repayment schedule. The downside of borrowing from your 401(k) is that if you lose your job, the loan must be repaid quickly, often within thirty days. To see if this is an option, consult your plan's documentation.

You may also want to consider using the funds in your IRA. Within the laws governing IRAs, you can actually withdraw money from an IRA, as long as you replace it within sixty days. This is not a loan, so you don't pay interest; rather, this is a withdrawal that you're allowed to keep for sixty days. A highly organized person could possibly juggle funds among several IRAs. But if you're one day late—for any reason—you'll be hit with a 10 percent premature withdrawal fee, and the money you haven't returned will become taxable.

Credit Cards: They're not terribly creative and they are definitely a last resort. But credit cards are quick, easy and allow you to keep ownership in your business in some cases . In the short term, they are also cheap if you pick the right ones. That is, a minimum payment of $50 per month can hold down a whole lot of debt. Of course, if you only make the minimum payment, your balance continues to grow, and if the business fails, you have to pay the piper. But if things go well and the business pays off the balances without missing a beat, then you look back at your early credit card financing with a nostalgic fondness, and perhaps a twinge of longing for simpler days. If not, you'll be holding a load of credit card debt that will remind you for years to come how costly it can be to start a business.

Friends and Family: Friends and family present a formidable source of capital. It is not unusual for friends and family to invest up to $100,000. However, investments with friends and family can turn out bad when things don't go as planned. The situation can be even worse than with professional investors because friends and family react to bad news as much with emotion as with logic. If you are going to borrow from friends and family, take the following steps to protect everyone involved:

- **Get an agreement in writing:** This will eliminate all conversations that start with, "You never said that . . .."
- **Emphasize debt (loans) rather than equity (ownership):** You don't want friends and family involved in your company forever. Before you

know it, they will start telling you how to run the place, and long-buried emotions will emerge. Make it a loan, and pay it back as fast as you can.

- **Put some cash flow on their investment:** If Dad says, "Here's $50,000. Try not to lose it, and pay it back as soon as you can," that's great. But consider paying some nominal interest at regular intervals so that the two of you have a reality check. It's better to pay this quarterly, rather than monthly. This way, when things are teetering, your lender won't immediately know it.

SBA Loans: While most banks, as well as select commercial finance companies, offer Small Business Administration loans, there are two specialized categories worth knowing about. These are certified lenders and preferred lenders, both of which have entered into contractual relationships with the SBA and officially participate in the Certified Lender/Preferred Lender programs (CLP/PLP).

These lender programs were designed to provide better response to borrowers; they accomplish this goal by placing additional responsibilities on the lenders for analysis, structuring, approval, servicing and liquidation of loans, within SBA guidelines.

About 850 lenders qualify for the SBA's Certified Lender Program, having met certain criteria, the most important of which, from the borrower's perspective, is extensive experience in SBA loan-guarantee processing. Certified lenders account for about 4 percent of all SBA business-loan guarantees. Since the certified bank does much of the SBA's work, the agency offers turnaround times of three business days for processing the application.

Approximately 450 lenders meet preferred lender standards. This group processes approximately 21 percent of SBA loans. Preferred lenders have full lending authority and, as a result, can offer a one-day turnaround on completed loan applications.

If you are seeking an SBA loan, your best bet is to work with a certified or preferred lender. The SBA-guarantee process is tricky, at best, and you want a lender who has been through it more than once. To find certified or preferred lenders, visit the SBA web site at www.sba.gov, or call your local SBA office for guidance.

If you are getting someone to finance, lenders require a comprehensive document that addresses their concerns about your financial needs and more importantly, your ability to meet your obligations. Be prepared:

- Know all of the components of your business plan.
- Anticipate any concerns and be prepared to address them.
- Rehearse your presentation and keep it simple and precise.

Angel Investors: Like treasure hunting, a lot of search and hard work goes into finding an angel investor, but once you do, the pay-off can be worth it. Angel investors (individual investors) help two different kinds of companies: companies still in the early stages with no revenue, and already established companies looking for expansion. Also, angel investors are appropriate for companies that have increasing product or service sales and need additional capital to bridge the gap between the sale and the receipt of funds from the customer. These individuals invest on three conditions:

1. The company's management team or owner has similar motives and style as the angel.
2. The company has a high quality, unique product or service that consumers want.
3. The company displays high growth potential.

But be careful. If you are looking for an angel investor, be prepared to give up some control over your business, because you will have to welcome outside ownership, and they can be hard to negotiate with. Plus, the cost is expensive—capital from angel investors is likely to cost no less than 10 percent of a company's equity and, for early-stage companies, perhaps more than 50 percent. In addition, many angel investors charge a management fee in the form of a monthly retainer.

Range of Funds Typically Available: $300,000 to $5 million.

Where They Are Located:

- Universities
- Business incubators

- Venture capital clubs
- Angel confederacies

The more technology-driven an area's economy, the more abundant these investors are.

How to Find Angel Investors:

1. Call your chamber of commerce and ask if it hosts a venture capital group. Many such groups have a chamber affiliation.
2. Call a Small Business Development Center near you and ask the executive director if he or she knows of any angel investor groups. Ask the SBA if you don't know where an SBDC is.
3. Ask your accountant. If your accountant doesn't know, call a Big Four accounting firm and ask for the partner who handles entrepreneurial services. Ask him or her to point you in the right direction.
4. Ask your attorney. Lawyers always know who has money.
5. Call a professional venture capitalist and ask if he or she is aware of an angel investor group.
6. Contact a regional or state economic development agency and ask if anyone there knows of an angel investor group.
7. Call the editor of a local business publication and ask if he or she knows of any groups. These professionals often write about such activity.
8. Look at the Principle Shareholders section of initial public offerings (IPO) prospectuses for companies in your area. This will tell you who has cashed in big.
9. Call the executive director of a trade association you belong to. Ask if there are any investors who specialize in your industry.
10. Ask your banker. If you do business at a small bank, ask the president of the institution. If yours is a larger commercial bank, ask your lender. If you do not have a lender, ask for a lender who works with loans of $1 million or less. A good small-business banker knows of such groups because companies that have received an equity investment are good candidates for a loan.

Downsize and Cut Back: An unfortunate solution, but if your business is in financial trouble, you need to save what can be saved. Before you lay anyone off, be sure you have looked at all the options, and talk to your employees. They might be willing to work with you to get the company back on its feet.

Get Creative: I watched expenses closely, used every penny as wisely as possible, and came up with creative solutions to get by. I had to get imaginative in new ways of increasing revenue, working out trade or payment plans with vendors, tapping into credit cards or lines of credit when necessary, and working another job when needed.

Finally, keep in mind that no business runs smoothly on a consistent basis; there are always going to be speed bumps on the road to success. You'll run short on cash at some point, and you will need to be creative to make it through. You never know what problems are going to pop up. Even though there was a positive response to my first camp, it struggled nonetheless. Reflecting back, I sometimes ask myself, "What problems *didn't* I encounter?"

Some days, I thought I would not survive another week, but I took my time and dealt with the problems by following my gut and doing research on an issue before I made a decision. If you look at each challenge as a learning experience to help your business grow, the outcome will override any negativity.

CHAPTER 12

Build Your Pack

As a new pup in a lawn full of bully dogs, it's important to surround yourself with the right people. I compare running a business to being a character in a video game. Villains, aliens, and monsters are always popping up to try and take you down. It helps to surround yourself with good people who can help you combat your enemies. Even though you have a great head for business, you might lack sufficient knowledge about legal, financial, purchasing, and accounting matters. Whether this is the case or not, who you choose as your advisors is essential in the stability of your company and your mission. When the pressure is on, it's important that your team has the ability to come up with the right answers to support you.

When hiring your team, invest your money in great people who are smarter than you. If you are financially able, make sure you have the right professionals on your full-time payroll. If you cannot afford a full support staff, at least hire or befriend a consultant to advise you on the start up of your business.

Consultants have played both a good and a horrible part in the growth of Camp Bow Wow. A good example is Scott, a business coach, who advised our management team for a year. He did a fabulous job of showing us the metrics we needed to examine and taught us some general management concepts that have helped us build our business. On the flip side, I utilized a professor from my master's program as a consultant to help our business grow, and it was a disaster. He fired several of our vendors that were key players in the franchise industry, ran up a $20,000 bill supposedly setting up a retail distribution chain for us (which never amounted to anything), and had my team running scared with his do-or-die antics.

On the financial side, we ran through four different highly recommended contract chief financial officers (CFOs) before we found our winner. They all took a very generic approach to our business and didn't take the time to learn about the nuances of accounting in franchising—and how important it is in forecasting to know the ins and outs of the revenue model of the business.

Consultants tend to think their knowledge and expertise will translate into effective feedback for the company they are hired to help, when in reality it takes years to understand the culture of an organization and the "whys" behind a lot of the things that go on.

If you decide to go the consultant route, here are a few tips:

- *Thoroughly* check references, and do your due diligence on projects they've completed.
- Start slow with a small insignificant project and let them prove themselves before you turn them loose on something bigger.
- Introduce them to all members of the team to make sure their personality and style will mesh.
- Set them up on a pay-for-performance compensation plan, not straight hourly rates, or project-based compensation.

Consultants played a role in the demise of my settlement as well. Consider my financial advisor. My uncle helped me research and interview the financial planners, and we picked a respected and well-known gentleman who put the majority of the money in variable annuities and variable life insurance programs. There was very little left liquid for me to live on, and I was not in any shape to be dealing with a new career or getting back in to pharmaceutical sales. As my rebound marriage unraveled and the custody battle set in, I had to start liquidating the investments that were performing horribly because of a shift in the stock market in the mid-1990s, and I was penalized for early withdrawal. It was a mess.

I was not emotionally involved in the management of the money, which was a *big* mistake! And honestly, I felt so guilty about getting it the way I did, I subconsciously didn't care if it went away. I was the "girl who got rich from the plane crash that killed her husband." It drove me nuts, since I was always so driven and believed I would make it on my own.

When it comes to money, it's best to do your own research before and during the time you are working with an advisor. An accountant, a lawyer, an insurance specialist and experienced mentors in your area of business are all key members of a great team to help you with your business. Utilize references from other people in your industry—or from key advisors that have proven themselves.

Develop relationships with various mentors who have traveled the business road before you. You've got to lean on others that know more than you who can help you manage the business. There is not enough time in the day to be everything to everyone. Get the right people to back up your bark and your bite. And, if you have the attitude that nobody can do anything but you, you won't succeed as an entrepreneur.

SCORE and SBDC are two great resources for entrepreneurs who are launching or expanding their business. SCORE "Counselors to America's Small Business" is a nonprofit association dedicated to educating entrepreneurs about the formation, growth and success of small business nationwide. SCORE is a resource partner with the U.S. Small Business Administration (SBA). The Office of Small Business Development Centers (SBDC) provides management assistance to current and prospective small business owners. The best part is they are absolutely free! SBDC is a government-funded organization that employs consultants and professionals experienced in helping business owners tackle typical work-related challenges. SCORE addresses problems in a similar manner, but their professionals are retired executives who are volunteering their time in a confidential environment to owners like you.

You need mentors to help you along the way. These individuals are essential in helping you and your business grow. My father is my greatest mentor and had the most influence on my sense of entrepreneurship and my ability to be successful in business. A salesperson all of his adult life, he demonstrated the ability to develop a relationship with his clients. He had great attributes of a leader, and I learned my gung-ho nature from him. He would listen, problem-solve, and always made the customer feel important. When he started his own business, I saw how strong his perseverance was, a trait I wanted to emulate. No matter how many hours it took, or how unscrupulous people would be, he stayed true to his vision and did the right thing, even if it was uncomfortable. My mom was a mentor for me as well, balancing my dad's entrepreneurial spirit and drive with cautiousness. She also knew the importance of doing your analysis before making any key decisions. Her level-headed nature was also the check and balance to my dad's entrepreneurial spirit.

Guidelines to Creating a Great Pack

Rule One: Have An Environment Where You and
Yours Can Bark Freely

I realize that, with my position as CEO, I set the tone for the company. This is both a privilege and a responsibility. Make sure you take care of your internal business family, and establish loyalty with your colleagues. If you treat your employees well, they will go above and beyond the job requirements to help you grow your company. As ambassadors of your brand, they need to feel proud and excited to be part of the growth of the company.

Care

The spirit of camaraderie is so rewarding when you show you respect the opinions of those working for you. It's the philosophy based on open relationships in the workplace that I hold dear.

Ask employees what they need to be more resourceful. Give them what they need in terms of freedom, time, resources, encouragement and rewards. Value creativity in employees more than preserving the routine, conforming, or playing political games.

Develop an organizational environment that stimulates and sustains original thinking. Respond to individual needs for creativity. Some staff want more challenging work assignments, not just more work. Others want more freedom in how they work. Others want to be left alone. Regardless of how you respond, help employees feel respected and connected.

Allow employees access to creative consultants and coaches. Provide financial support for employees to develop through formal education, continuing education and professional associations.

Share

In living through Bion's very public death, I became a very open person. This trait carried over into my leadership style, which also incorporates open communication. Very little is said or done behind closed doors, and most company information is common knowledge among the staff, which serves to keep confidence high among workers in a small business. It also encourages employees to feel like their contributions are critical to the success of the company.

People always tell me not to be so open about everything, including details about the business, my concerns, money, etc. I tried for a while to be more businesslike and closed up, but it's not me. What's wrong with people knowing how you feel? I understand where they are coming from. It's true that you are vulnerable when you are open about your business and your life. But in the end, it builds a tremendous amount of trust with people and you learn a lot about what people really think. They don't hold back when they feel like they will actually be heard if they speak up. I am outgoing, trusting and love hearing an outside viewpoint. So when it comes to being businesslike, I learned to be myself, but to set boundaries to protect myself a bit. If the conversation is critical, being frank opens things up, and that's how things get accomplished.

Creativity is contagious, so encourage communication among staff through Internet-based staff directories, mentoring programs, cross-department work teams, and social events. Quickly disseminate new ideas through publications, leadership development programs, strategic planning meetings, and recognition events.

Call for proposals about new ideas. Allow employees to compete for committee assignments, work projects, and jobs. Allow for participation in decision-making.

Forthrightness

When you are running the show, there is no time to be polite, shy, or to fear negative feedback for your openness. A forthright approach may be harsh at times, but in the end, it is more effective. It's tough to tell people the truth about how you feel, especially when you are dealing with the ones who are closest to you. It was hard for me to approach family and friends who worked for me because I was always afraid to jeopardize my relationship with them if I didn't agree or approve of their performance. I would try everything I could to make it better, or to put them in a position that might work better, rather than tough it out and deal with the root issue. Once I learned to be straightforward with them, however, it became much less of an issue, and we all knew where we stood.

We are living in a society where all of us strive for acceptance and want to be liked. People don't like being told you don't agree with them. I think it's a key to why women have a tougher time leading. We are brought up to believe we have to take ownership of problems and solve them, and we have to be gracious and happy while we deal with other people's problems. In the end, it's always easier to just say it like it is and deal with the fallout, rather than tiptoe around an issue and drag it out.

Some people that work for me or my franchisees, are taken aback when I go from being lighthearted and friendly to a tough, toe-the-line leader who holds them accountable. People either go the confrontational route or the defensive route until they know me well enough to go toe-to-toe with me and stand up for their opinion. I've lost some of them because they didn't like it, but most respect me and like knowing where they stand with me as the head of the business.

Rule Two: Hire Slowly, Fire Quickly

You have heard it before for a reason: Bad hires will only hold you back and waste precious energy and resources. A solid piece of advice my parents gave me was to surround yourself with great people. I have a smart team that is as passionate about dogs as I am, and equally as concerned with safety. That's made all the difference with how I run my business and foster my work ethic among my team. You are only as strong as the team that backs you up.

We've grown as a family organization. My family has always been involved in my business, and my original franchisees were instrumental in helping us grow. We are all very passionate about the dogs, and about building our business. That passion must also include a devotion to dog-related causes. Camps participate in foster dog programs and get involved in local animal-related charities. We have a "start up" mentality and allow flex hours, bringing your dog to work with you, and mandatory volunteer hours each month for the foundation. It's a fun and very rewarding environment, so it's not too hard to get that work ethic out of people. I tend to hire people that are equally committed and excited about helping us grow our brand.

I would say, generally, not to hire help until you absolutely can't stand the workload any longer. Having a staff is so time-consuming and overwhelming emotionally, and you've got to be ready for that. You also have to be ready to give up the attitude that "It's quicker and better to just do it myself." When you are ready to hire, make sure to check all references and ask them for actual data and reviews from their past life. How did they specifically accomplish certain achievements? Not how their *team* did it, but how *they* did it. In the beginning, it's easy to hire the young and inexperienced because of their vivacious energy and enthusiasm. But keep in mind that one good employee equals three or four greenhorns.

There are a few key people in my life who I have considered my good friends *and* business partners. You may find yourself already looking into your pool of friends to become part of your team. Who do you trust with your money? Who has compatible business ethics and qualities similar to your own?

Be wary of getting family and friends involved and assuming that because they have good hearts and are interested in your business, that they'll have the skills to do it. If possible, you should avoid hiring loved ones. If not, better make sure they are damn qualified—not just for the job at hand but to grow with the company. It's important to be surrounded by knowledgeable people who have great skills, not just people who love you. I have learned these lessons the hard way. It's unfortunate when you trust someone close to you and they betray you.

Jim Collins, in the book *Good to Great,* talks about letting someone go at the first sign in your gut that it's not going to work out—the first sign you have to micro-manage them to get work done. I don't take quite that harsh of a stance, but often, if I look back at the fires, I knew pretty early on who needed to go. Evaluate the good and bad of having them continue working there. If the bad outweighs the good, then cut your losses and move on. Drama will drag you and your company down so *always* try to let someone go in a positive, business-oriented way. A bitter, frustrated ex-employee today may be your formidable competitor tomorrow.

Rule Three: Accept Personal Accountability

The only time you should be pointing the finger is when it is facing you. In one-way or another, I am responsible for all the adversity that has been thrown in my path. I have come to learn, in overcoming both personal and professional hurdles, that I cannot achieve anything by blaming others. I learned this the hard way because I experienced so much heartache and trouble when I didn't accept my own involvement in a situation. Once you do, it brings the walls down—it brings a coming of the minds on the issue.

Taking responsibility for poor decisions, financial woes and other challenges has prepared me for the trials presented by the conception and growth of an industry-leading company. *Only promise what you can deliver, and always deliver what you promise.*

If your company is not where you want it to be, the worst thing you can do is to make excuses or unjustly blame others who are trying to help you. It is obvious the highs are easier than the lows, but as leader of the pack, you cannot let your insecurities come off in a rash and abrasive way.

The "Golden Rule" is the epitome of professionalism—always treat others as you would like to be treated. Whether it's an employee, a client, or even that strong-willed franchisee who always knows a better way to do things! I always try to put myself in other people's shoes.

Rule Four: Commit to Being the Best

Committing to being the best means two things: Being the best you can be for your company, and your company being the best to its customers.

Camp Bow Wow was founded to improve the lives of pets everywhere by promoting good health and socialization. So, naturally, everything we strive to accomplish is centered on this goal. Our most fundamental principles and procedures are based upon the highest levels of pet safety and customer service, thereby raising the standards of an entire industry. You only have to look to our competition, or nearest dog boarding facility, to see our impact. Our customers recognize our commitment to excellence and take comfort in knowing that this commitment is present in every Camp Bow Wow and Home Buddies from coast to coast. For this reason, we are heads and tails above the rest, and the clear leader of the pack!

Focus on "how." We stood by our brand and business and focused on being the best for our customers and for the dogs. Dov Seidman wrote the inspirational guide *How*, focusing not on why or when, but the significance of "how" we do anything, and this means everything. Touching deep into the realm of human behavior, how makes all the difference in your decisions and overall business. You are building a business in a sea of competition. No matter how efficient, fast or innovative you become, your competition is fast at your heels, thinking of ways to be better. We are constantly driving to differentiate from one another, to be elected as the top choice from a customer. However, there are very few areas we can move where others will not copy. Don't concentrate on outshining your competition, concentrate on *out-behaving* your competition. Focus on the inside, and don't let the outside throw you.

Being the best means doing what's right for your company, as opposed to satisfying your personal needs. Since I started Camp Bow Wow, I have been committed to the growth and stability of my company. In terms of monumental success, I take a modest salary, but then plow the rest right back into the business. As a business owner, to take a little, you need to give a lot. Fast growth equals big requirements for capital. You need to be prepared to devote your life and time to your business—eat, live and breathe it. But you definitely need to incorporate balance, too, which I discuss in later chapters.

I have sacrificed many personal needs and time with Tori, my friends, and family for my passion. Not to mention a much higher paying job and weekends and holidays! Every risk takes a level of sacrifice on your part. If you are not prepared to put in the effort, then you are not in the right spot to support the needs of the business. A half effort will fail every time.

Naysayers

There will always be a group who will disagree, or always have an opinion about what you are doing with your business. With Camp Bow Wow, some local veterinarians didn't believe in socializing dogs, due to the shortage of any existing research. There was a huge lack of confidence in our ability to handle and screen the dogs. One obstacle was veterinarians not understanding this new concept, and the other barrier was a lack of similar facilities. Other vets were stuck in their old ways and afraid the success of Camp Bow Wow would hurt their boarding business.

I took it upon myself to change their minds! It took building relationships with them and bringing them to the camp to see how happy the dogs were! It took a huge amount of effort on our part to try and persuade non-believers. Enough of their clients were coming to camp, so they eventually opened up to the idea.

Leave the naysayers behind as you forge on with your dreams!

Betrayal

It cuts deep when you find out you're being cheated, and when it turns out to be someone you care about, well, that's just putting salt on the wound. On more than one occasion, I found out that a friend of mine was either not trustworthy, or was stealing money from me. These were people that were supposedly "helping out."

The first experience I had was dealing with the $1 million settlement I received from the plane crash. Many people asked me to "help them out," or asked to borrow money. Some were friends, a scarce few were family, but very few paid me back. It taught me a lot about setting boundaries and expectations with people. This was the main reason I started my second company, The Maginot Group, because I knew there were others in the same predicament.

Then, when I started Camp Bow Wow, I often turned to family and friends for help with the business. As I discussed earlier in the book, my good friend and first business partner was my first wrong turn with family and friends. Two years into our working relationship (ten years into our friendship), I found out that she was embezzling money. It was heartbreaking.

I hired another friend who I had known since seventh grade, to help me in Colorado as my executive assistant. After two years of working together, however, I had to fire her after she got drunk at our franchisee annual meeting and didn't show up for work the next day. She was in charge of the meeting for 200 people. This was the second time this had happened, so I had to let her go. If I hadn't, it would have set a horrible example for my staff.

And there have been other dear friends lost over money and business, as well. Over the years, I have come to learn that it is so hard to have your friends work for you because many will blur the line between business and pleasure.

In a nutshell, my advice is to be careful who you do business with. I attribute my hiring mistakes to the fact that I trust people—a lot. This is a characteristic that has steered me into dangerous water. Sometimes I feel like I have to share my good fortune, and I get flooded with guilt at times for the wonderful success I've had! But I will tell you now that I have done this for the last time. I'll be hesitant to loan any money in the future.

Even though my learning came in a rough package, I feel like all of these lessons I've learned about money since Bion died have been my training wheels for when I deal with any money matters. I had to learn not to be so trusting and to hold my cards closer to my vest. I also partially hold myself accountable for a lot of the problems. For example, allowing my friend/ business partner too much freedom with my books and the business overall. I could have blamed her for a lot of the issues we experienced around the business when I had to fire her for embezzling, but I took responsibility for not being involved enough and for trusting her too much.

Part III
JUST DOGGONE
DO IT!

CHAPTER 13

Feel the Fur and Do It Anyway

Once you have completed your brilliant business plan (you entrepreneur, you!), there is undoubtedly some fear that creeps into the minds of everyone starting a business. Let's look at some common concerns:

You have a great concept, but feel that you aren't the one to bring it to life. You may not feel capable, but you really want to start your own business and you can't drop the idea. This kind of conflict can stop you from taking *any* steps forward. What do you need to feel capable? If you decide that you have a personal weakness (e.g., you're disorganized or are scared of numbers or networking), take one initial step that will boost your confidence. What suits you?

You love to spend time embellishing your dream business in your head, but haven't yet taken a hard look at it because you're afraid it won't hold up. What if your vision has to change or won't work at all? Sometimes we're afraid to take something apart, in case we can't get it back together again. But finding one or more aspects of your business that might not work is a chance to make positive adjustments at the drawing board. Trust in your own creativity and problem-solving skills. Talk to someone close to you to get their reaction, and don't be afraid of their suggestions.

Maybe you suddenly feel you aren't really the "entrepreneur type" or that you'll seem foolish to others who have more experience. Remember that many successful entrepreneurs felt this same way early on. Spend some time focusing on your strengths. It may help you to know that almost every successful woman entrepreneur has said she feels like an "imposter"—even though she was already successful in her business. So you're definitely not alone, feeling the fear and wanting to do it anyway!

This is too much like work! Well, yes. You will need to learn, develop skills, and put them to work. If you have chosen a business that fits you, though, the rewards and the fun you are looking for will come along as well.

The hardest part is not the decision, but the leap itself. It's a feeling reminiscent of your first day on the playground, conquering the slide. You see the object, it looks fun and exciting, and you want more than anything a successful ride. So your hands grip the metal rods, and with each step, that hole in your stomach gets larger and larger. The moment your backside hits the cool metal, you look down and the slide seems endless. Could you fall off? No! Your certainty for success beats out the fear of the unknown, and you slip down that slide with that indescribable feeling of elation. If you can bring back the courage you had as a small pup, than you can definitely conquer starting your own business!

Think Outside the Cubicle

Think of your favorite business owners and their success stories. They seem to have it all together and you want what they have. Why not you? You seem to have all the goods to be the pick of the litter. There are many entrepreneurs who are just chained to the desk when their spirit is in starting a new venture. Why do they stay? The security of a job has a lot to do with it. I understand there are many factors within each story that prevent one from making the giant leap into starting a business. Find the courage! You know you have a problem if other people are asking you regularly, "So, have you quit your job yet?"

Your job may be the equivalent of a jagged splinter you can't get out, just painful enough to bear. You need to know yourself and become your own biggest fan in order to really control your own destiny.

Remember that first day of school when your teacher asked everyone to make a name card, and you could not wait to get out those markers? You carefully displayed your name on that cardboard with specific colors and shapes that you thought represented you the best. You sat back and admired how you represented yourself proudly. Would you take the same amount of pride in representing yourself now? Take out a piece of paper and write ten things you like about the job or career that you are in right now. Is one of them stability, the fact that you're receiving a paycheck? Or is it the typical adage, "I'm lucky to have a job"? How about taking control of your own luck!

Keep in mind that *this is your life*. I will tell you right now, your boss is not going to pop up with a smile and say, "Hey you! Guess what? I just read your mind and I think it's a great idea to start your own business. You were meant to do it! In fact, let me give you double your annual pay as a parting gift!"

One of my favorite slogans is Nike's "Just Do It." These three words could not be simpler, but have so much meaning. Know your capabilities and get into a routine of not only thinking about doing it, but actually *doing it*.

The brain works in mysterious, but also predictable, ways. In order to get results, you must practice putting your thoughts into action. The more you consistently do something right after thinking about it, the more rapidly it will become stored in your mind, and your body will become familiar with taking charge. Your brain responds to repetition, so start with everyday tasks. Hey, don't you have to do that load of laundry? Go into the laundry room right after you think about it. What about writing those thank-you cards? It seems simple enough, but the more you get into the habit of accomplishment, the harder it will be to resist acting on bigger thoughts and dreams. Sometimes we get too bombarded with everyday demands and needs that we forget to put our take-charge behaviors into action. It isn't that you don't have that fire in your belly, because you do—you just need to spark it back up.

You have to believe in what you are doing and you need a huge vision. Always think *big*. When Tori was a baby, I would sit her down and ask, "How big are you, Tori?" She would chuckle and stretch out her little arms as wide as they could go to where I nodded in agreement and say, "So big!" It isn't about your age, weight, or physical size in the world. It's about knowing you can achieve big things and be big in your own right.

Face Your Fears, Then Turn Your Back on Them

As with personal life choices, all types of fears can come with being an entrepreneur—fear of having enough faith in yourself to have financial stability, to manage employees, to relinquish control over management, and ultimately, the fear of failing with the associated pressures of employee, franchisee and vendor livelihoods. All of these fears are based on very real concerns, but all must be controlled in order to forge ahead.

Channeling the skills I acquired from enduring hardship has helped me overcome the fears that presented themselves along my road to success and the growth of a successful business. The key is how to clarify and focus your vision, thus tuning out the fears that threaten to hold you back. The difference between the people living fulfilling lives and the people with lackluster lives is *how they respond to fear.*

Fear of Succeeding

Sometimes we don't commit to our goals because we're *making* ourselves not commit, or always falling short. This type of fear is different than fear of failure or the unknown, because it mostly happens unconsciously. We all have a built-in mechanism for risk analysis to decide if we "think" we can succeed or not. With information and knowledge, the brain gets more confident about succeeding. It's similar to leading someone through the sales process—the objections, or "no's," are just steppingstones to getting a "yes." We work the same way when we evaluate the possibility of succeeding.

> *"People who lack the courage to act will*
> *always find a way to justify their lack of action."*
> **—Mark Twain**

Someone overcome by this type of fear procrastinates instead of perseveres; they "wait for the right time" to make a go of it. It's never too early, or too late, to start your business. If you have all the incentives and means to start, then go ahead and start. You could always wait until you get married, or own a house, or have kids, or whatever. How about living in the present? Stop the excuses! The most successful people evaluate an option, make a decision, and decide it will work. They are usually successful *because* they are so decisive that that's the way it will be (law of attraction)!

The fear of success hinders us for various reasons. In order to figure out if you fear success, you need to ask yourself, "What will happen if I succeed?" The real fear might lie in the side effects of succeeding, and not success itself.

Reason #1: Success brings you power, money, and presumed happiness. You may have witnessed someone warp and change under these conditions. Prosperity can easily bring out the demons, and you're afraid your character will spoil—that you'll become someone you don't want to be. You fear that your friends, acquaintances, and those you hold most dear will envy you, push you away, and possibly take advantage of your power.

> **Check it:** Know your integrity will not let your character succumb to such negative traits. Your antidote for this type of fear: Believe in yourself and the people around you. There will be people who disappoint you, who get greedy and ugly. Believe me, I have seen this dark side of people. It's the quality in the rest that make up for the few bad apples.

Reason #2: The amount of change that comes with new affluence and the strains on your schedule. You second-guess yourself and doubt you'll be able to juggle everything at once when you reach the top. You're going to be on the move, traveling constantly, and always pressed for time for your loved ones and yourself. You think, "If that's what I have to sacrifice for success, I don't want any part of it."

> **Check it:** Take it from me, there *will* be a strain on your schedule and you *will* have to do some juggling. But it is not impossible! More to follow on work/life balance!

Reason #3: If you succeed once, then you're expected to continuously succeed by employees, colleagues, friends, family, customers—and so and so forth. Once the bar is raised, you cannot slip under.

> **Check it:** Unfortunately, more often than not, we have insecurities. This brings up doubt concerning our capabilities. If you succeed once, it means you're doing something right, so keep at it! As long as you hold

strong to your mission and keep the promise of what your company delivers, there will be continuous support.

From the list above, how many of these fears have you felt? These thoughts "camp out" in the subconscious mind, so now make a *conscious* effort to take precautions against them. It's natural to feel nervous of what's to come, but you should feel excited as well! Offset those doubts with uplifting thoughts—know you *can* succeed in your dreams, and with success comes more positive ways of thinking. Success means you can delegate, but only after overcoming the fear that nobody can do anything but you. Focus on how you can take better control of your life through success. Examples include getting a maid to come in once a week, paying for a gardener to fix those overgrown shrubs, or buying ready-made dinners at Trader Joe's, or elsewhere, instead of slaving in the kitchen. These luxuries bend your schedule so you can spend your time more effectively. On the business side, it means hiring great people who know more about their part of the business than you do, and who also buy into the vision.

Fear of the Unknown

Dipping your paws into the business pool comes with the uncertainty of not knowing how deep the water is. We all fear what we do not know, but there really is no need for it to be this way. Throughout history, the unknown usually equaled danger.

Now, the population is still vastly scared of the unknown because you can't confront problems until they are a reality. It's about control, and you feel safe when you have more of it. The funny thing is, though, that you actually have more control when you accept that life happens. This acceptance helps us admit we don't control most of life's challenges, and we have to learn to roll with the punches. How to control is simply how to respond to the punches thrown at us.

Fear sneaks up on you when you are down, adding on to your doubts and insecurities. You can either attack or surrender, and when you attack, you turn into the leader you want to be. After all, fear does not happen when things are well-organized and planned out. Move into uncharted territory by using fear to your advantage.

Why Not Start Exploring Now?

Channel Christopher Columbus, Lewis and Clark, Robert Peary—be an adventurer today and cross your own map of the unknown. Obviously, number one on the list is starting your business, but here are other ways to conquer the unfamiliar:

- Make a list of fears and confront them. If you're afraid of water, go scuba diving. What about heights? Travel to the tallest building in your city.
- Try out a new hobby or activity. Find something that interests you, but that you know nothing about. What about taking karate lessons, or hang-gliding? You might uncover a new love that you would have never known if you didn't try.

Now is the time to rustle up your fur and be courageous! From my great childhood friend Molly, one of my favorite quotes: "Worry is a debt you may never have to pay." Bion's plane crash made me confront the unknown. For the first time in my life, I had no control. I couldn't make Bion come back, and I couldn't change what had happened. I could only choose how I responded.

Fear of Failing

Fear of failing plagues the actual execution of expanding your idea into a solidified result. When you put yourself out there, it takes a giant risk, a risk that may produce failure. In turn, doubt creeps in and acts as a barrier for taking the next step. The key is acknowledging the possibility of failure, which makes taking a risk seem less scary and debilitating.

Instead of a stumbling block, let failure become the steppingstone on the road to success. It's necessary and possible, but you have to *learn* from failure and integrate these lessons for it to be worthwhile. No one wants to be put in the position of losing, but if you hinder yourself to this fear you will never change your life.

- Picture yourself in the worst-case scenario. Do you have it? Now, visualize yourself solving it and overcoming it. It's a part of life; you are not taking risks if you never fail.

- Have the same mentality as the persistent salesperson. You know that you've got to get ninety-nine "no's" before you get one "yes," and that each "no" is a step closer to "yes"!
- Take each failure as a lesson learned so you can take necessary precautions to avoid the same actions next time. Integrate your lessons learned into your business to make it better.

Keep in mind that many successful entrepreneurs have faced failure to get to where they are now. By seeing that obstacles are inevitable, you can forge ahead with the certainty that it's going to work out no matter what.

Accepting failure is essential in growth. It's maturity; it's realizing that it's only the end of the world if you let it be. It helps you understand that the road to success is not straight—it's a crazy ride! Part of the feeling of accomplishment when you hit your goal is to know you didn't give up when things got really tough.

You have a choice to make each day—live or die. You can grow and learn and live your life to the fullest, or you can recoil and turn inside and not grow. Making mistakes is part of growing and learning. Failures are just steppingstones—challenges to teach you so you can make your company even stronger.

When Failure Is Not an Option

What makes failure not an option? When you decide it isn't! My contingency plan was not to give up, but to keep starting companies until I did succeed.

The timing to start Camp Bow Wow was perfect. I was ready to devote myself to a business I loved, and I felt I had no choice but to succeed. So, failure was not an option!

The plan was taken down from the shelf with the help of my brother, Patrick. He saw me struggling to try and find my niche and a way back to a happy, fulfilling life. He knew my passion all along had stemmed from dogs, and he had seen how excited I had been in the past about launching Camp Bow Wow. He approached me one day and said, "You and Bion wanted to start that doggy day care center. You need to do that, and I'll help." For me, this comment was a form of personal awakening. Trapped in my emotional kennel, he gave me the extra push I needed to brush myself off and make Bion's and my dream a reality. I dusted myself off and tore away the cobwebs from the business plan that Bion and I first started. I was a working, single mom who had nothing left from the large settlement except a variable life insurance policy that was losing value. So I rolled the dice, and with the $83,000 I had left, I invested everything I had, including a lot of sweat equity, into the start of the first camp.

Learning from Failure

The aftermath of Bion's death lead me to some poor decisions, but how I rose from the ashes is what I pride myself on. Confronting so many struggles at such a young age made me fearless. If I could live through that (which at times, I didn't think I could), I could live through anything—any loss, any change, any fear. I hit rock bottom spiritually and had to dig deep to figure out what I truly believed. I read and read and read for inspiration. Books about death, grief, God, religion, you name it. Books were the outlet for my evolving emotions, and they bound my thoughts and feelings together to make me strong.

My first two tries at starting a business were not successful in the traditional sense, but they taught me so many lessons I needed before I could make Camp Bow Wow a success. It's all a mindset. I tried starting Nursery Works, thinking I knew plenty to make the business work. I got hammered. I didn't know enough about cash flow management, about the catalog business, about financial statements. At one point, I recognized that it wasn't my true passion, and I wanted to take my lessons learned and start a business I enjoyed more. So I shut it down. It wasn't a failure in my mind—even though I spent $250,000 and two years of my time. I learned a tremendous amount about starting a business and running a business. I took those lessons and started The Maginot Group. And that didn't work out either.

But I picked myself up, refocused my energy and headed down the path again with one more "learning experience" under my belt! I just kept taking steps toward my dream. And so should you—no matter where you are in the process of living out your own dream.

A top dog has to be quick and fearless in the decision-making process. Life is too short to play it safe with your choices. The line is extremely delicate because you have to think big to win big, but you also have to be smart about it. A cheesy, but effective, anecdote is to live each day like it would be your last. You miss out on what you might win if you only focus on what you might lose.

89

This Means Taking a Risk!

"The greater danger for most of us is not that our aim is too high and we miss it, but that it is too low and we reach it."
—Michelangelo

Taking a risk might seem scary because of the level of uncertainty. My staff told me I was crazy when I started spending $20,000 a month on advertising in the airline magazines. We didn't have the money to risk at the time, but I did it anyway and it paid off! We sold a ton of franchises off of the ads, and the investment was more than worth it.

Other Good Risks I Took:

- I started franchising with no money. Luckily enough, it took off quickly and the franchise fees coming in helped fuel our growth!
- I started my second camp before the first one was profitable—it ramped up quickly so it broke even within a few months.
- I turned away investors at various points in my journey who likely would have tried to take over the business. I stuck it out on my own and still own 100 percent of my company and retain control.

Here are some things you can do to make taking risks more palatable to you:

- Establish cut-off points to indicate the limits beyond which you will not go.
- Maintain control by delegating risk and responsibility, rather than simply exercising your authority.
- If you encounter failure, take responsibility for it, decide what went wrong, and take the necessary corrective steps.
- Obtain the necessary financial and human resources to deal with risk by being willing to share the potential rewards with others.
- Reduce the intellectual and financial sides of risk by using other people's brains and other people's money.
- Never adopt the attitude that, "I'll make this work if it kills me." Also, don't ever encourage it in those you work with.

Instead of trying to avoid risk, seek it out. Weigh the possibilities for gains and losses. And when the odds seem to be in your favor, move boldly ahead. As they say on the sports field, "No pain, no gain."

Decisions, Decisions, Decisions

Read about any successful inventor or businessperson and you will inevitably notice something: A habit of decisiveness in all that they do. What is decisiveness, exactly? It is a word we often hear, but rarely define. In simplest terms, decisiveness is accepting the fact that you are in control of your own life. It is the methodical, systematic effort to determine the best course of action and then carry it out. Put negatively: It is the refusal to let the random gyrations of society, chance, and whim set your course. Psychologist Michael J. Hurd sums up decisiveness as "trusting and acting on the conclusions of one's mind."

Obviously, decisiveness is a quality entrepreneurs stand to benefit from enormously. So how can you develop this habit in your own life?

Hurd offers some practical tips on being decisive in his article, *"What Should I Do?"* When stuck with the question, "What should I do?" don't stay stuck. Don't fall prey to the temptation of blindly asking someone else what you should do. Instead, ask yourself—and answer—the following questions:

- What are my options in this situation? (If there is only one option, your question is already answered. If there are two or more options, then proceed to the next question.)
- What are the likely immediate and longer-term consequences of each option? (Make a list of each set of consequences and confine the lists to one page.)
- Which options are the most desirable and the least desirable, and why?
- What is my final choice? (If you cannot answer this yet, then first develop the top two or three finalists. Then go to a final judgment.)

Questions like these will become invaluable guides to action: Which supplier should I use? Do I believe this cost is legitimate? Is this deadline realistic? Do I have too much on my plate?

Of course, it will be far easier to ask yourself those questions if you accept that you are the author of your own destiny. As appealing as this sounds, few of us ever fully accept what it means in practice. Hurd elaborates more on this helpful point, which is essential to creating a lifelong habit of decisiveness:

> *"This exercise is an example of using your own rational judgment instead of letting others tell you what to do. It's the alternative to both do-as-I-say dogmatism and do-as-I-feel subjectivism. It's called being objective. Some don't like the idea of objectivity because it seems too cold or harsh; others feel it's too hard, or too much work. What's the alternative? Self-defeating impulsivity? Doing what a dictator tells you to do? Praying to the skies and hoping for an answer in code? Get real!"*

If you work at it, you can stop yourself as you are about to fall into these traps. Do you find yourself thinking, "Ahh, I can't be bothered with this now; I'll cross the bridge when I get to it"? Or how about, "I know this is important, but it's just such a big decision that little old me can't possibly decide it." If you think these thoughts, drop what you are doing and change them. Successful entrepreneurs cross bridges miles ahead of them in their own minds and are better off for doing so. They do this by asking themselves, "If I don't decide, who will?"

So, instead of succumbing to those passive thoughts and letting them move you, take a different approach. Will yourself to sit down and consciously decide the pressing questions before you. If you need to write a business plan, don't think , "Oh my God, this is such an important task that the slightest little error will screw it up. I might as well not even try." Instead, put on a pot of coffee, sit back, and do some research. Read a few sample business plans. Get some expert advice. And then, sit down and write one. It doesn't have to be perfect the first time, and you can certainly go back and edit it. The important point is that by doing this, you have made the decision to move forward. You have gone from thinking to doing.

This same thinking applies to any decision you face. Instead of getting stuck in analysis-paralysis, calmly think about what this decision requires of you. One way of staying calm is to remind yourself that no matter what you are doing, someone, somewhere, has done it before. It may be challenging, but it is doable. You can also save yourself a lot of mental anxiety by asking, "Where do I start?" Once you figure this out, the rest tends to unfold naturally.

Above all, keep your cool and always remember that you are in charge. If you resolve to make this a part of your outlook, it is almost impossible to fail.

Former Chrysler chief and American business icon Lee Iacocca, now in his eighties, once said, "Decisiveness is the one word that makes a good manager." Iacocca recently spoke to The Associated Press about the concept of decisiveness and how he sees it. Here are some excerpts from the interview:

- On America: "There's a little bit of the cowboy mentality — bring in the Marines, Teddy Roosevelt. When we do something, we do it quickly. We're decisive. I think it's embedded in the culture a bit."
- On changing your mind: "What is wrong with changing your mind because the facts changed? But you have to be able to say why you changed your mind and how the facts changed. Or the press will cream you—and possibly rightfully so."
- On being at the top of the heap: "In a corporation, there can only be one guy in the end: the CEO. And that's what the president of the United States is, really—that rugged individualist who has that power . . . .You're the guy. You're responsible. It is a tough job, let's face it. It really is a tough job. They really have to become Superman."
- On decision-making experience: "I always go back to people that I thought were decisive to find out what they did for a living. I always go back to Harry Truman: Should we drop an atomic bomb to save 100,000 lives? That's a hell of a decision to make. Did he make that decision by himself? No, he had advisers."

The Leadership Sniff Test

This test is designed to distinguish the doers from the dreamers. When meeting with would-be entrepreneurs, I can gauge their chances of success within a few moments, based on several less-than-scientific, but nonetheless accurate, criteria.

Did they reschedule the meeting more than once?

If they did, this usually means they are not committed to following through with their vision. If they are going to waste time by canceling or rescheduling, it's a sign that they will treat others around their business the same way.

Time is an individual's most valuable resource—especially that of a mentor or fellow business owner.

Did they show up on time?

Respecting other people's time speaks to how seriously they are taking their venture. No need to be early, just punctual. In a day's span, it's hard to accomplish everything necessary to launch a business. If you are unorganized or unprepared, it reflects on how successful your business will ultimately be.

Are they prepared?

How do they know what questions to ask or how to utilize the precious time a potential mentor has granted them if they are not prepared? It's like getting ten minutes with the president of the United States. Wouldn't you have your questions prepared ahead of time so you could glean the most possible out of that time? The folks who have wowed me had a clear vision of their business, what they needed help with, and how I could help them achieve their goals. Half the battle is knowing what you want from the person you are meeting with.

Are they humble?

> "The chief executive who knows his strengths and weaknesses as a leader is likely to be far more effective than the one who remains blind to them. He also is on the road to humility, that priceless attitude of openness to life that can help a manager absorb mistakes, failures, or personal shortcomings."
> —John Adair, quoted by Henry O. Dorman in
> The Speaker's Book of Quotations (1987)

What is your tendency when someone starts explaining something you think you already know? Do you interrupt to make sure they know you already know what they want to talk about? The next time this happens, try something new—listening. Let them finish their explanation. Probe for more detail. You might be surprised and discover something you did not already know. You might walk away with more knowledge than you would have had you interrupted them to stroke your own ego.

Humble leaders assume they do not know all the answers and allow people to explain things to them. They look for the opportunity to learn something new, and they use every opportunity to make others feel valued. Humble leaders know the world around them is changing faster than they can keep up, and they are grateful for the opportunity to learn something new or to reinforce knowledge they might already possess.

This is not to say that you need to act stupid to be humble. There is no harm in someone walking away knowing you are knowledgeable, so long as the process did not leave them feeling "less than you." Sharing your wisdom is important, but it must be done in a way that "lifts the other person up."

In the act of being humble, you make others feel important and valued. That is the gift of the humble leader. Focus on your humility and you will find it can lift a weight from your shoulders. It takes a lot of effort to pretend you know it all. Besides, it is more refreshing being around people with some humility. Arrogance gets old fast.

Did they listen and ask questions during the meeting, or did they talk the majority of the time?

We should all know that listening, not talking, is the gifted and greater role, and the more imaginative role. And the true listener is much more beloved and magnetic than the talker. And, he is more effective in learning and accomplishing. So try listening. It will work a small miracle, perhaps a great one. How can you learn and grow if you are constantly talking?

I get frustrated when someone wants to meet with me about his or her business idea, and then spends the entire time espousing the great benefits of their business. If they need me to validate their business, then it's not one that will probably work. The point of meeting with mentors or other business professionals is to learn from them—learn what worked and what didn't in creating and growing their business. Otherwise, I assume the person thinks they already know everything, and I'm not much good to them. Thus, it's a waste of everyone's time.

Are they organized and detail-oriented?

These traits are necessary because the bank, your investors and your clients will all expect detailed and organized reports from your business. You also can't reach goals or stick to a plan if it's not well articulated or laid out—all of which requires organization. You can show you have these traits by having a well-prepared and detailed business plan, presentation, and a list of prepared questions. Also, knowing your metrics and business goals will be vital to your discussions with other professionals about starting your business.

Are they fearful or hesitant about starting the business and, if so, are the fears rational concerns about having the funds, or do they center on self-doubt?

Over the years, I have received many calls and scheduled meetings with people who expressed interest in launching their own companies, who then did not even bother to follow through with set appointments. This reeks of future failure and dreams of businesses that will never even make it to the business plan stage.

Others show up and boldly pitch their dreams without listening to the reality of my experiences. There's no value to such meetings, and there likely won't be much to the business if would-be entrepreneurs neglect to soak up the advice of those who have gone before.

One business owner I met with wanted to franchise his upscale, men's-only hair salon. He was realistic, goal-oriented, and asked all the right questions, but his one worry was that he lacked access to enough cash to make his dream of growth a reality. Despite this concern, he passed the sniff test. His fear was based on a very real stumbling block to growth for many small businesses—a lack of capital.

Conversely, a woman I talked with once wanted to launch an adventure travel company. Our talk revealed that she was unfocused and had little confidence in what her brand would represent. Additionally, she underestimated the time commitments the new business would require and assumed her connections would do most of the work. She had little money to invest and assumed her "smarts" would trump the need for money. By the end of the meeting, I was mentally holding my nose.

Your first and last impression can either make you or break you in a professional sense. It is said that within three seconds someone has a definite impression of who you are. This just shows you how important it is to come off strong and assertive when you are networking or meeting with other professionals. When you give off a great first impression, you establish a strong rapport. This neurological support is beneficial because it shows you can be trusted, even when the brain is quick to perceive a threat. Smile and grasp firmly when you shake their hand. If you are seated, always stand when he/she enters a room, and seem genuinely pleased to be meeting with them. These are simple little things that seem irrelevant, but that will prove you are capable and have proper social etiquette.

You can lead even if nobody believes you have what it takes. I was told over and over that without a tremendous amount of working capital, and the backing of a larger franchise, I would never survive the path to a successful franchise brand. My tenacity and belief in myself helped me to overcome these warnings. I liked being the underdog, the runt of the pet and franchise industries. Taking on industry giants, like Petco and PetSmart, was a challenge I thirsted for. Being the runt is an advantage; no one expects you to succeed or make a difference. When you do, and do it repeatedly through leadership, it will move you from the runt to the head of the pack.

You Need to Be Competitive

Many start-up businesses fail due to the inability to keep up with the competition. Most industries are built on copycats, one person has an innovative idea and others copy it to create a niche. Therefore, a top dog needs to have a thriving competitive nature to keep up with the high standards of the market. Never underestimate your competition, and at the same time, never underestimate your own abilities and intelligence.

When I opened up Camp Bow Wow, the competition was small. But since I have changed the industry, others have come along to try and copy our services. We don't let ourselves get distracted by other business opportunities that come in our direction, and we don't try to be everything to every dog owner. I am a perfectionist, and have been very specific about what the rules are and what the brand is, and that really led the way for franchising opportunities. But we are constantly evolving based on the learning experiences and opinions of our franchisees, and I think that helps us stay ahead of the competition.

I recently heard a great business consultant talk about a conversation he had with the head of Coca-Cola. He asked the gentleman, "What's your secret to success?" The head of Coca-Cola replied confidently, "Pepsi!" Every morning, each and every Coke employee receives an update on Pepsi's market share and stock price. The employees then rally around their great brand and prevent an ounce of market share slide to the "other guys." Americans love a battle—we thrive on having an enemy—whether it's Iraq, China, or Russia. It's no different when it comes to business. And, boy, do we have an enemy in our Camp Bow Wow world! There is only one company that offers the standardized, consistent message that we do, with a national presence: PetSmart.

In a research note upgrading PetSmart (PETM) recently, Standard & Poor's Equity Research noted, "While we expect a slowdown in consumer spending to impact sales of discretionary pet supplies, we continue to believe underlying demographic trends for the industry remain very strong." Good news where bad news is rampant. And what's good for PetSmart, is good for us!

At Camp Bow Wow, we should feel confident that the good news about growth at PetSmart is ours for the taking! PetSmart has recently shifted its mission from being the top seller of pet food to helping consumers become better "pet parents." Along with making their 928 retail locations homier and hosting pet parties, they have been busily rolling out blue-shingled pet hotels (kennels) in their stores. They feature private suites with raised platform beds and TVs airing shows from Animal Planet for $31 a night, as well as "bone booths," where pets can take calls from their owners, and porous pebble floors where dogs can pee—all at an extra fee, of course. The hotels, along with services such as grooming, training, and in-store hospitals, have helped PetSmart expand its service business from essentially nothing in 2000 to $450 million (which includes grooming and training), or 10 percent of overall sales, this year. They claim to be "a revolutionary alternative in pet care . . ." They even copy our tag line by using, "It's the best place to play—or stay when you're away!" Straight from their web site, "Our Doggie Day Camp is available to provide all-day play and exercise in our fully supervised play rooms."

I look at it this way: If our brand and concept were not first class, do you think a multi-billion dollar player in our segment would be inspired to copy it?

As an entrepreneur, you must be agile and able to outsmart the stodgy corporations that delay in making adjustments to their strategy. You must learn to trust your instincts, take risks, and react quickly when making decisions about your business.

Stick to Your Gut

It took me many years and lots of mistakes, including doing what others wanted me to do, rather than listening to my gut, before I was successful. Some of my mistakes included:

- Investing all of my money into retirement vehicles, rather than starting Camp Bow Wow in the beginning.
- Spending big money on advertising the "experts" recommended, when I knew in my heart how to reach my customers best.
- Bending to my various franchisees on issues that I knew in my gut shouldn't be touched, such as the layout of our camps, our logo, our equipment and chemicals.

I often believed others knew more than me about how to run my various businesses or handle my investments based on their supposed experience and education. In all reality, my instincts were usually right-on about what I should do. I typically did a lot of research and learned in my own way before I made a decision. I gained confidence and started to experience more success when I did follow my instincts. Ralph Waldo Emerson said it best: "Self-trust is the first secret of success."

I still listen to others and contemplate their advice, but I rely on my own experience and expertise to make a good decision. Perking up my ears and getting other people's perspective helps me think outside the box. Gathering information, analyzing it quickly and efficiently, and making a firm decision are key. Getting as much buy-in as you can from your team and your organization is critical. When you roll, don't let naysayers move you off the goal. Stick firm to your decision until you have reason to question it. When that moment comes to second guess, you have to be willing to question those decisions and correct your approach at the first sign of trouble. Rely on your gut and instinct, but also be quick on your feet when you see danger ahead.

> *"The right way is not always the popular and easy way. Standing for right when it is unpopular is a true test of moral character."*
> —Margaret Chase Smith

My two grandfathers were both great business inspirations for me. On one side, my grandfather was a West Point graduate and a successful private executive. The other was a chemist and engineer who had the ability to problem solve, whether it be a chess game or the invention of a new technology. They were both enormously successful in life and taught me a sense of doing what's right, not what's easy.

The smartest business move I have ever made is the complete ownership of my company. I own 100 percent of my franchise company, and am proud to have stuck it out, even when easier opportunities, such as selling, arose. When hard financial times are weighing you down, it's very easy to be manipulated by outsiders vying for your company. Even though it might seem they have your best interest at heart, keep in mind that they are highly skilled in the art of persuasion. There is a reason they come forth at times of struggle. Being your own inner coach will help you deal with the pressures of outside sources who are trying to change you to fit a certain mold.

- A business, much like a relationship, is a series of compromises. The advice is congruent to both cases; never compromise to the point where you lose yourself. You pick and choose your battles; a lot of times people back off if you just give them a small win. Try to win the war, not the battle.

- Consultants are notorious for coming into companies like a bull in a china shop with recommendations for change. It takes years to understand the complexities of any business and to be able to effectively address issues. Take what they say with a grain of salt.

- If your business is struggling to the point of having to sell, don't do it alone! Find a highly recommended business attorney or investment banker to help you. It's a very complex and confusing process.

CHAPTER 14

Signs You're on the Doggone Wrong Trail

If you start a venture only to lose interest before reaching the company's potential, big, lighted warning signs should start flashing in your head. The signs will be telling you to turn back and take another path because you are on the wrong one.

Since there are a large percentage of small businesses that do fail, it's useful to understand the reasons why this happens. In the pool of failed and successful businesses, it's important that you have a business initiative that is on the right path. If your business plan has cracks, you need to know where they are. With these key indicators as your life preserver, you will be able to successfully swim on top of the water, as opposed to sinking to the bottom.

Reason #1: Lack of Preparation

Every good idea must come with the right support to make it profitable. That support stems from the business plan, which is proof of a prudent entrepreneur. Many failed businesses are attributed to the lack of a winning proposal. Whether you are considering seeking a franchise, buying a business, or starting a small company, lending or investing individuals will only consider an investment after a thorough review of your project.

There are many templates and off-the-shelf programs that can be purchased for your assistance. However, they are all basically the same, with the following sections needed for an adequate proposal:

- **Executive Summary:** A succinct overview of what is included in your business plan. Although these pages are placed first, it is common and useful to write this section last.
- **Company Description:** An in-depth look at how all the elements in your business fit together. It is helpful to begin with a mission statement explaining what your company is all about.
- **Products or Services:** This section is dedicated to a thorough explanation of your products or services offered, and how they compare to those of your competitors.
- **Market Analysis:** A comprehensive description of your market, customer needs and identification; where you will fit in; and your competition.
- **Marketing and Sales Strategies:** After you identify your market, you explain your strategy on promotion, product placement, costs of distribution and production, and how you measure effectiveness.
- **Organization and Management:** Identifying the legal structure of your business, such as a sole proprietorship, C corporation, S corporation, etc. You will also identify who your key players are, their responsibilities, and how much they will be compensated.
- **Financial Data:** A compilation of all your financial statements. At the very least, make sure you include a projected profit-and-loss document, along with a statement of cash flow. It is also wise to show a break-even analysis, balance sheet, and an income statement.
- **Funding Request:** Depending on what your financial plan is, this is the section in which you request funding for your business. If you do not need outside funds, you can leave this section out.

Reason #2: Wrong Incentive

I found my search for career success to be as trying as dealing with the grief of Bion's death. In the following years, I attempted to travel down a shaky road filled with a number of failed ventures and unwise financial decisions.

Still, in pharmaceutical sales, I thirsted for more, and my original dream to start my own company was always sticking out in the back of my mind. I tried to keep myself occupied and kick my life into the busy, work-filled viability I had always wanted. Along with my volunteer work as a puppy raiser for Canine Companions, I started my first entrepreneurial undertaking. Having just had Tori, I saw an opportunity when looking for baby bedding sets for her. I followed a quick, fleeting gut feeling and started a baby bedding company without a solid business plan.

That was the first warning sign: Never spawn a business based strictly on research alone. Nursery Works was a mail-order catalog company that sold baby bedroom sets. The business launched well, but quickly fell apart due to the constricting circumstances of my inability to juggle the add-ons to my life. *The second warning sign started flashing: If you feel the inability to put your all into your new venture, cut your losses.* I felt like I had a million balls on my nose that I had to balance, but I felt compelled to do something with my life, even though I wasn't ready. I was dealing with the personal turmoil of losing Bion, being in a dysfunctional rebound marriage with an alcoholic/drug addict, and juggling the role of being a new mom. It was a disaster, to say the least.

My next start-up business was the consulting company, The Maginot Group. This company aimed to help people deal with sudden wealth and was centered around having to deal with a personal loss and the acquisition of large sums of money at the same time. Sudden Wealth Syndrome is very common. It occurs when people experience a lot of guilt over receiving money through a sudden financial windfall. Seventy-five percent of people who receive over $500,000 from a settlement blow it within three years. If I had an MBA and couldn't figure this out, then I knew other people couldn't. I had been through every mistake you can make with the money, but I lived to tell about it and hoped to help others avoid the same mistakes.

I began taking classes on investing and received my financial planner's certification. I marketed my firm as an objective source of information and help in dealing with the financial aspects of sudden wealth from an inheritance or lump sum settlement.

My firm did not sell securities or manage money, but it helped clients evaluate their financial health and goals, estate-planning needs, and options for hiring professional help, such as whether to use a stockbroker or a financial planner.

It also provided them with an overview of stocks, bonds and other investment options and helped to formulate a plan of action. In many cases, it also helped client's interview and hire advisers, and it provided them with references to seasoned planners, estate-planning lawyers, accountants and grief counselors.

People needed a safe place where they didn't feel like there was a second agenda when venturing into the shark-infested waters of having money. I found it rewarding to be able to sit down and understand where these people were coming from. There is a huge sense of freedom because you have all this money and have all these choices, but it can be paralyzing. Early on, though, I realized it was me who needed the guidance. *So the warning signs became quite obvious. I was unknowingly looking to others who found themselves in my unfortunate position. I wanted to learn how they were able to swallow the pill and right themselves.* It also became very frustrating advising people who didn't always listen and who made the same mistakes I did. So I pulled the plug.

Are you dealing with a financial windfall?

For those who are dealing with a sudden death or financial windfall, take one minute, one hour, and one day at a time—baby steps. Follow your heart. While you should listen to the advice of your friends and family, do what is right for you. Try not to do what others think you should do, do what you feel is right, even if it's not the easy road. Also, take a year off if you can and don't make any major decisions, business launches or purchases. It's so hard to do, but so important. And finally, take care of yourself emotionally and physically; your body is your strength and your source of wisdom through the process.

I am a firm believer that with every mistake comes a new lesson to be learned. With the development of The Maginot Group, I did learn that I loved public speaking. I often spoke to CPA and CFP groups about how to help their clients through the issues surrounding sudden wealth syndrome. It was very rewarding, especially after 9/11, when I was able to help the survivors and families who were dealing with these issues. But ultimately, I started the company for the wrong reasons.

Reason #3: Not Enough Cash

Business analysts report that poor management is the main reason for business failure. Poor cash management is probably the most frequent stumbling block for entrepreneurs. Understanding the basic concepts of cash flow will help you plan for the unforeseen eventualities that nearly every business faces.

Cash Versus Cash Flow

Cash is ready money in the bank or in the business. It is not inventory, it is not accounts receivable (what you are owed), and it is not property. These can potentially be converted to cash, but can't be used to pay suppliers, rent, or employees.

Profit growth does not necessarily mean more cash on hand. Profit is the amount of money you expect to make over a given period of time, while cash is what you must have on hand to keep your business running. Over time, a company's profits are of little value if they are not accompanied by positive net cash flow. You can't spend profit; you can only spend cash.

Cash flow refers to the movement of cash into and out of a business. Watching the cash inflows and outflows is one of the most pressing management tasks for any business. The outflow of cash includes those checks you write each month to pay salaries, suppliers, and creditors. The inflow includes the cash you receive from customers, lenders, and investors.

Positive Cash Flow

If its cash inflow exceeds the outflow, a company has a positive cash flow. A positive cash flow is a good sign of financial health, but is by no means the only one.

Negative Cash Flow

If its cash outflow exceeds the inflow, a company has a negative cash flow. Reasons for negative cash flow include too much or obsolete inventory and poor collections on accounts receivable (what your customers owe you).

If the company can't borrow additional cash at this point, it may be in serious trouble.

What Are the Components of Cash Flow?

A cash flow statement shows the sources and uses of cash and is typically divided into three components:

- **Operating cash flow:** Operating cash flow, often referred to as working capital, is the cash flow generated from internal operations. It comes from sales of the product or service of your business, and because it is generated internally, it is under your control.
- **Investing cash flow:** Investing cash flow is generated internally from non-operating activities. This includes investments in plant and equipment or other fixed assets, nonrecurring gains or losses, or other sources and uses of cash outside of normal operations.
- **Financing cash flow:** Financing cash flow is the cash to and from external sources, such as lenders, investors and shareholders. A new loan, the repayment of a loan, the issuance of stock, and the payment of dividends are some of the activities that would be included in this section of the cash flow statement.

How Do I Practice Good Cash Flow Management?

Good cash flow management is simple. It involves knowing when, where, and how your cash needs will occur. It also includes knowing the best sources for meeting additional cash needs and being prepared to meet these needs when they occur, by keeping good relationships with bankers and other creditors.

The starting point for good cash flow management is developing a cash flow projection. Smart business owners know how to develop both short-term (weekly, monthly) cash flow projections to help them manage daily cash, and long-term (annual, three-to-five year) cash flow projections to help them develop the necessary capital strategy to meet their business needs. They also prepare and use historical cash flow statements to understand how they used money in the past.

It's necessary to begin with the end in mind and important for entrepreneurs to set their sights on a goal line, whether it's financial or not. For me, it was a psychological barrier I needed to address, but my main focus was the fun of starting a brand and building a company. Camp Bow Wow has been so challenging and such a learning experience—every day is an incredible adventure!

Financially speaking, I have successfully crossed the $1 million revenue mark with my business. I had my eyes on the monetary prize when I formed my business plan. I wanted to make the $1 million back that I squandered from the plane crash settlement. I have always felt tremendously guilty about that, and I wanted to prove to people that I could make it on my own without a handout. I have often heard, "Well, she's successful because she got all that money from the crash, and had that to start her business." That could not be further from the truth. I only had $83,000 left when I started Camp Bow Wow, and I worked a pharmaceutical sales job for the first year the camp was open.

All in all, think of your definition of success: Is it monetary, personal, growth? If it is monetary and not meaning, you can get trapped in the "golden paw cuffs." Your business will have no purpose besides financial pleasure. And believe me, that is short-lived.

It is easy to get trapped by the golden paw cuffs when you have everything people assure you will make you happy—big paychecks, nice cars, a big house—and you just cannot find the will to get out of bed in the morning. You just know something is lacking, and if you are an entrepreneur, or are aspiring to be a great leader, it is likely this shortfall is simply a new challenge to master.

Women specifically find it difficult to focus on their own needs and build the confidence to break from a corporate job and test their entrepreneurial bones!

One woman I met was with a global cosmetic company and had her high-level management position cut due to a restructuring. At age fifty-five, she had become accustomed to a rather rich existence during her employment, but that lifestyle didn't come without high expectations from her employer. The layoff became a blessing in disguise as she shifted the hard work and skills she had developed in the workforce to opening her own day spa. Without being laid off, she would not have taken the risk because she had it "so good." Now she realizes that "so good" is having control of her destiny and building her own future.

Job "push factors" may be spurred by job dissatisfaction, job loss or change in life circumstances. Ultimately, it may not matter which force got you going. What does matter is whether you understand how to harness that force and make it work for you.

How to Get Back on Track if You Started on the Wrong Paw

There are examples of entrepreneurs who choose to look past the warning signs and get themselves in an even deeper hole. An acquaintance of mine espoused passion for her dream of creating a small business to fill a niche she believed needed filling. Unfortunately, she decided to launch her new venture with a huge debt load and no working capital to see her through the lean first years. Moreover, she became extremely defensive any time I would suggest that she may want to take a step back and spend more time planning before launching the business. To date, she is still struggling and desperately needs investors to keep her company afloat, but still refuses the advice of those who have been in her shoes before.

Stop and re-evaluate what your vision is and what your passions are. You're wasting your time and resources if you keep plowing ahead. Get back to basics and ask yourself why you are starting a business. What about it is so appealing? Then dig in and really think about how you want to spend your days, your life. Visualize your day-to-day life if you move forward with the business. Does it feel fulfilling and exciting? For me, the answer lied in Bion, my dogs, and my original dream of launching Camp Bow Wow, the one business no one thought would work, but the one about which I felt most passionate.

If you feel panicky after doing some self-reflection and examining your business skills, don't be alarmed. It is good to question your capabilities at this point. Your fears will make you look more closely at what you *need* to do, not just what you *want* to do. As an entrepreneur, you'll have to commit to doing some hard, but satisfying, work. You'll have an easier time if you are realistic. Confidence can help, but it should be *informed* confidence.

CHAPTER 15

Specific Challenges of Being a Woman Entrepreneur

This chapter will be specifically focused on my challenges as a woman entrepreneur, and lessons other women can learn from my experiences. Guys, if you want to keep reading, there are definitely some takeaways for you, as well!

What does it really take to be a great woman leader or business owner? We've inherently got what it takes. Our leadership style is innovative, trusting and empowering—and ideally suited to today's business challenges.

Nevertheless, we all know the "glass ceiling" statistics: Only 6 percent of top executives in Fortune 500 companies are women, despite occupying 40 percent of all managerial positions. Only 3 percent of Fortune 500 CEOs are women, and only 3 percent of women-owned firms have revenues of more than $1 million, compared with 6 percent of men-owned firms.

However, statistics are not proof that women can't be powerhouses in business. Quite honestly, a woman and a successful business mogul seem to go together as smoothly as peanut butter and jelly. We can take care of other life forms, have astonishing intellects, social grace, and we have a remarkable aptitude for taking charge and taking names. We can do it all!

The Rise of the Female Entrepreneur

If we're talking statistically, let's look at some positive studies from the Center for Women's Business Research:

- Women own 41 percent of all privately held U.S. firms.
- Nearly 10.4 million firms are owned by women (41 percent), employing more than 12.8 million people and generating $1.9 trillion in sales.
- For the past two decades, the majority of women-owned firms have continued to grow at around two times the rate of all firms (42 percent versus 24 percent).

Banking and Finance Relationships

- Women business owners' satisfaction with banking relationships has more than doubled since 1992 (35 percent versus 82 percent).
- More than two-thirds (67 percent) of women business owners choose financial products and services based on their relationship and experience with a lender.
- Women business owners who obtained capital persevered, making an average of four attempts to obtain bank loans or lines of credit and twenty-two attempts to obtain equity capital.

Characteristics of Women Business Owners

- Women business owners are prepared to face risk: Most (66 percent) are willing to take above-average or substantial risks for business investments.
- Women and men business owners have different management styles. Women emphasize relationship building, as well as fact gathering, and are more likely to consult with experts, employees, and fellow business owners.
- Women owners of firms with $1 million or more in revenue are more likely to belong to formal business organizations, associations or networks than other women business owners (81 percent versus 61 percent).

Exit Strategies of Women Business Owners

- Women and men business owners are equally concerned about price when selling their business.
- Women owners who plan to sell are more concerned than their men counterparts about the buyer's identity, personality, and background (72 percent versus 39 percent), the buyer's plans for the business (79 percent versus 52 percent) and plans for current employees (86 percent versus 61 percent).
- Women business owners are nearly twice as likely as men business owners to intend to pass the business on to a child (37 percent versus 19 percent).

What Glass Ceiling?

The female population largely influences business as noted above. The statistics espouse the danger of being in the group that doesn't succeed, which make up the majority. But to move forward, you need to focus on the group that has succeeded.

Take it from a woman who's defied all those numbers—with the right strategies, attitudes, and "been there, done that" coaching, women can break right through that glass ceiling. Following are some tips on keeping up in a man's world:

1. Be less expressive and less emotional—act as if you were the calm, cool, CEO of the company, even on the way up!
2. Dress in a manner that is not overly feminine, but rather more conservative, and dress the part of a top executive.
3. Watch your voice: Lower your pitch and strengthen your tone.
4. Don't be humble: Assertively take credit for your accomplishments.
5. Find a woman role model, and a man role model, and mentor high up in your organization.
6. Be heard in meetings. Voice your opinion. Be confident, but not overbearing.
7. Ask to be rewarded by objective results, not by hours at work.
8. Get social—make the commitment to do the social networking to move up.

9. Identify and reveal your team's inner strengths—help them help you look good.
10. Select a company/industry that has a track record of promoting women!

Putting the POW in Female Empowerment

As women, mothers, and business owners, we must make important decisions daily. When it comes to our career, our philosophical outlook on life affects how we embark on each day. It's often too late before people realize they've played into the dog-eat-dog culture that is habit forming and negative. My advice to businesswomen everywhere is to hold on to your convictions and beliefs. Women often feel they must sacrifice parts of themselves to fit into the ruthless business world, but that kind of workplace philosophy can be very detrimental personally and professionally. I have found that sticking to my basic ideals contributes to my success. I know that I am doing this for my family and for the betterment of pets everywhere.

Today, while many women are gaining the strength to pursue the dream of starting their own business, they need encouragement to advance themselves. With hard work and perseverance, the greatest of challenges (whether personal or professional) can be conquered. It is vital for women to network with fellow promising entrepreneurs. You'll need the inspiration, the friendship, and the advice. Plus, it's energizing and uplifting to surround yourself with positive, powerful females.

The More We Know, the More We Can Grow!

There are so many easily accessible reference tools out there for business-oriented women and young professionals. As women in the business world, we need to be each other's support systems. What a powerful breed we are! Take this opportunity to tap into our wonderful community of powerful businesswomen. Just think of all the knowledge, experience, and inspiration residing in this community of millions.

Angela Jia Kim, a New York businesswoman, recently started her new online networking company that is geared toward female entrepreneurs. She describes SavortheSuccess.com as a mix between Facebook and Linked-In. Now, females can find common ground and a supportive community all from the convenience of their computer.

Other Online Resources:

MyBiz for Women (www.sba.gov/women)

Run by the Small Business Administration, this microsite provides insight on issues relating to female business owners and entrepreneurs.

Online Women's Business Center (www.onlinewbc.gov)

The SBA's Office of Women's Business Ownership (OWBO) provides services, tools, and resources, including counseling on related business subjects.

Women-Owned Businesses Selling to Government (womenbiz.gov)

This site specifically targets women business owners interested in starting a business relationship with the federal government.

Women Entrepreneurship in the Twenty-First Century (www.women-21.gov)

Here, women can find information necessary to put their dreams into realization. The Department of Labor and the Small Business Administration are two of many partners contributing to this resource, which focuses on helping small businesses get an equal advantage to big businesses.

SCORE on Women (www.score.org/women_resources.html)

Women can peruse an extensive list of links to other women-related businesses on this website.

Women's Small Business Research (www.sba.gov/advo/research/women.html)

Here, the Office of Advocacy offers a source of economic research for small businesses.

re:Invention Blog (www.reinventioninc.blogspot.com)

Kirsten Osolind writes this interesting blog, highlighting tips and tricks of the trade.

Passing the Torch

We can always strive to help each other open doors, minds, and opportunities. With the state of the economy as it is, now is a better time than ever to support each other's dreams!

It's incredibly important to me to talk to young girls and grow their self-esteem. Watching me grow my business has instilled a great work ethic in Tori and has taught her about self-esteem. We recently tested a program with our local Girl Scouts to teach young girls about business. We had them write a business plan for their own dog programs and decide how to market them. And, they had to manage the dogs for a while at one of our camps.

I'm very involved with young entrepreneurs and work to champion other women entrepreneurs. I'm also part of a CEO support group called Vistage. There are twelve of us in the group and we meet for a day once a month. It's extremely valuable, but I am the only woman in the group. So I also have an informal group of women who I meet with in Denver to share professional successes and disasters. Women are just so much more open to that type of dialogue.

Powerful Women Role Models

Raised by a powerful female myself, I grew up idolizing successful women in the world. By looking at our fellow female leaders, it's proven that giving back is equally as important as getting to top dog status. Here are some of my favorite female forces dominating their industries and the world:

The Baking Bigwig—Debbi Fields

A woman from humble beginnings, Debbi Fields holds the name to one of the nation's most successful, and well-known, dessert empires. Few women can see their name become such a successful symbol and live to enjoy such acclaim as the leader of the Mrs. Fields cookie empire.

The cookie mogul explains her start: "I was really happy being a housewife, I was proud to be there for my husband, but it did not necessarily make me feel great." After craving something more, her entrepreneur appetite kicked in, and she turned her passion for chocolate chip cookies into a multimillion-dollar enterprise.

With absolutely no business experience or support from her family, Debbi was relentless in pursuing her dream. She pitched her business concept to a bank, a concept that had never before been attempted, and showed little promise on the surface. The bank accepted, and she opened the doors to Mrs. Fields Chocolate Chippery in 1977. Now, Debbi has moved from managing one shop, to being the first lady in baking, with over 600 franchise stores in the U.S. and in ten foreign nations.

Debbi's business ethics and values have remained consistent since her first shop opened in Palo Alto, California. By focusing on the quality of the product and excellent customer service, her reputation has stood unwavering.

- *"The greatest failure is not to try. Had I listened to all the people during the course of my life who said, 'You can't. You'll fail. It won't work. You don't have . . . .' I wouldn't be here today."*

- *"You have to have passion when you're finding a recipe for a career. If you love what you are doing, you'll never work a day in your life."*

- *"I learned how important what I call 'try and buy' was. I didn't want to advertise and say my cookies are the worlds' best. It would be presumptuous of me to say that. Instead I wanted people to actually experience the product, try the product, and if they thought it was worthy, if they liked it, then they could buy it."*

- *In response to her husband questioning her financial objectives: "Oh my gosh, Randy," she told him. "You know, I've got an annual goal. I've got monthly plans. But today I just want to get started. I just want to open up the store."*

- *"Good enough never is. Set your standards so high that even the flaws are considered excellent."*

—Debbi Fields

The Industrious Icon—Oprah Winfrey

She's been pegged "the most influential woman in the world" for her status, values, and acute business sense. Oprah Winfrey was the first African-American woman to become a billionaire, and ranked the most philanthropic African-American of all time. Her numerous endeavors and titles include: talk show host, Emmy award winner, media mogul, book critic, chairman, actress, and magazine publisher.

Oprah clearly states her corporate mission for *The Oprah Winfrey Show* " . . . is to use television to transform people's lives, to make viewers see themselves differently and to bring happiness and a sense of fulfillment into every home."

Her power and hold over the market has impacted the American culture to such extremes that she's been publicly assessed to be more popular than the president. But it's her philanthropic efforts that really set Oprah apart. She is the epitome of a powerful, successful, woman—focusing her mission on giving back and never straying from this purpose. Born in rural poverty, Oprah has overcome extreme hardship stemming from a childhood of sexual abuse. Her passion to help others has changed lives, changed perceptions, and transformed a culture.

It is no wonder that millions of aspiring woman entrepreneurs admire Oprah Winfrey for her entrepreneurial skills, business achievements, and commitment to philanthropy.

- *"As you become more clear about who you really are, you'll be better able to decide what is best for you—the first time around."*

- *"If you want to accomplish the goals of your life, you have to begin with the spirit."*

- *"Do the one thing you think you cannot do. Fail at it. Try again. Do better the second time. The only people who never tumble are those who never mount the high wire. This is your moment. Own it."*

- *"Follow your instincts. That's where true wisdom manifests itself."*

- *"I am a woman in process. I'm just trying like everybody else. I try to take every conflict, every experience, and learn from it. Life is never dull."*

—Oprah Winfrey

The Cunning Conservationist—Anita Roddick

This crusader founded The Body Shop, and used the stores to promote and shape ethical consumerism. Her belief was that businesses could have "moral leadership" and still be economically profitable. Anita was one of the first to promote fair trade with third world countries, and prohibited the use of animal testing with cosmetic products. A huge environmentalist, she became involved with Greenpeace and The Big Issue, and was highly active in campaigning for social issues. Her work on numerous causes included fighting for rain forests, voting rights, anti-sexism, debt relief for developing countries, anti-ageism, and the list goes on. A woman with unconventional ideals, Anita was a highly visible executive in Britain.

She started with twenty-five products, with five sizes of each product. From hand writing each of the beauty product labels herself, to setting up a franchise system—an eccentric move at the time—Anita made her dream for The Body Shop a reality. And although she admits there were trying times, she now just refers to them as "lovely anecdotes."

- *"If you do things well, do them better. Be daring, be first, be different, be just."*

- *"I want to work for a company that contributes to and is part of the community. I want something not just to invest in. I want something to believe in."*

- *"I hope to leave my children a sense of empathy and pity and a will to right social wrongs."*

- *"To succeed you have to believe in something with such a passion that it becomes a reality."*

- *"Be nice, for everyone that you meet is fighting a harder battle."*

—Anita Roddick

The Shrewd Saleswoman—Estee Lauder

This fearless entrepreneur was the only woman listed in *Time* magazine's "20 Most Influential Business Geniuses of the Century." By combining tenacity and keen intellect, Estee Lauder changed the face of the beauty industry with her unique marketing style and quality products.

Before she had her own office or laboratory, Estee whipped up her beauty recipes in her kitchen. With a low operating fund and no money for promotions and advertising, she had an inventive approach in marketing her product—place it directly in the hands of the consumer. A born saleswoman, she knew the product would sell itself. She was seen in every subway station, hotel, and salon, giving free demonstrations and makeovers to women. These simple, revolutionary moves quickly grew her client base and soon thereafter, she became a prominent name in department stores everywhere.

From the burner of her own stove to a global household name, Estee Lauder's success is a shining example of how taking a risk can pay off handsomely.

- *"If you have a goal, if you want to be successful, if you really want to do it and become another Estee Lauder, you've got to work hard, you've got to stick to it and you've got to believe in what you're doing."*

- *"When you stop talking, you've lost your customer. When you turn your back, you've lost her."*

- *"If there is a message at all, it's probably that we have to recognize in ourselves how we feel morally about certain things and make sure we follow that up with our actions."*

- *"If you put the product into the customer's hands, it will speak for itself if it's something of quality."*

- *"Touch your customer, and you're halfway there."*

—Estee Lauder

As the stories above exemplify, most successful women entrepreneurs possess the following traits:

Ambition: A successful woman entrepreneur is extremely ambitious, has an inner urge or drive to transform an idea into reality. Relying on experience from her previous tenure as an employee, educational qualifications, or lessons learned from an inherited business, she is ready to seize opportunities, set goals, possess clear vision, step confidently forward, and is ambitious to succeed. Every successful woman entrepreneur is truly determined to achieve goals and make her business flourish. In-depth knowledge of the field is essential to success. She comes prepared with new innovative solutions to old problems.

Confidence: A successful woman entrepreneur is confident in her ability. She is ready to learn from others, and to seek help from experts if it means adding value to her goals. She is optimistic and is willing to take risks. A successful woman entrepreneur uses common sense to make sound judgments when encountering everyday situations. This is gleaned from past experience and knowledge acquired over the years. She understands that it is essential not to get frustrated and give up when you face obstacles and trials; this is a part of setting up any business venture. The ability to explore uncharted territories and make bold decisions is the hallmark of a successful woman entrepreneur. A successful woman usually loves what she does. She is extremely passionate about her tasks and activities. Her high energy levels motivate her to contribute immensely toward building, establishing and maintaining a thriving business.

Open and Willing to Learn: A successful woman entrepreneur keeps abreast of changes, as she is fully aware of the importance of evolving changes. She is ahead of her competitors and thrives on changes. She adapts her business to changes in technology or service expectations of her clients. She is curious, interested to learn, and accommodates innovations.

Cost-Conscious: A successful woman entrepreneur prepares realistic budget estimates. She provides cost-effective quality services to her clients. With minimized cost of operations, she is able to drive her team to maximize profits and reap its benefits.

Values Teamwork and Loyalty: She has the ability to work with all levels of people. She is keen on maintaining relationships and communicates clearly and effectively. This helps her to negotiate even sensitive issues easily. She is empathetic to people around her and possesses good networking skills that help her to expand contacts and make use of opportunities.

Ability to Balance Home and Work: Cautious of not becoming a workaholic, a successful woman entrepreneur is good at balancing diverse aspects of life. Her ability to balance work with the family, combined with support from spouse and family members, enable her to blend business priorities with family and household responsibilities efficiently and effectively.

Feels Responsibility to Society: A successful woman entrepreneur is willing to share her success with society. She is committed to help others and enjoys doing it.

A woman can choose self-owned business as her career choice, provided she is to ready to: face the challenges that lie ahead of her, walk the extra mile, and rely on her own vast resources and abilities.

CHAPTER 16

Don't Forget to Stop and Sniff along the Way

An important premise of this book, while presenting the story of a start-up and encouraging entrepreneurship, is finding balance. For me, this means leaving the office at 3 pm to pick up Tori at school; fitting in an hour with my personal trainer twice a week; and taking the time to play with my dog and hang out with my husband. It means having a fulfilling personal life, even if that means fitting in work at 10 pm or 5 am. The concept transpires into my conception of leadership as a manager. Respecting the time and personal lives of my employees has helped me grow a team of dedicated and passionate people, who strive to make the company succeed. I harp on my staff to: "Turn off the Blackberry and the computer. Have a great family life, along with business." You can pay people less money if you offer them a better quality of life. All of my staff work from home a few days a week.

Work/life balance is a consistent challenge, but one I make a priority. I believe that happy employees are more productive. Therefore, encouraging balance throughout life will only better our work environment. When someone needs some time to go take a walk with their dog, attend their child's recital or take a day in the mountains, I encourage them. I find that allowing this flexibility actually motivates everyone and more gets done. When my staff does go overboard on the work side, I am the first to let them know it does not make me happy or impress me when they work ridiculous hours or ignore their family and friends; it makes me frustrated and sad. When there is balance, account- ability and commitment, performance increases and negative attitudes, stress and turnover decrease.

So how does one handle all the stresses and challenges of starting a business while having a life, too? We've all heard it before: "Multi-tasking gets you everywhere—and nowhere!"

Multi-tasking has become something of a heroic word in our vocabulary. Many executives pride themselves on their ability to "multi-task." Recent job descriptions that I've seen even ask that potential employees have the ability to multi-task. Multi-tasking is actually deceptively counter-productive and costly when we attempt to engage in it.

When most people refer to multi-tasking, they mean simultaneously performing two or more things that require mental attention, such as spending time with family while researching stocks online, or trying to listen to an employee while responding to an e-mail. What most people refer to as multi- tasking, should be referred to as "switch tasking."

Neurologically speaking, we cannot do two things at the same time. What we're really doing is switching back and forth between two tasks rapidly— typing here, paying attention there, checking our "crackberry" here, answering voicemail there, back and forth at a high rate.

Each time we switch, no matter how quickly that switch takes place in our mind, there is a cost associated with it. It's an economic term called switch- ing cost—and the switching cost is high. Switch tasking as a mode of working leads to:

- Stress
- Anxiety
- Short attention span
- Dropped responsibilities
- Productivity and focus problems

Steps to End Switch Tasking

Here are a handful of beginning steps to help slow down the switch tasking in your life and start finding some balance:

1. Take Control of Technology

Your cell phone ringer (even on vibrate) doesn't need to be on all the time. You can turn off e-mail notification on your computer as well. Become master over the nagging beeps and buzzes by creating some silence.

2. Create Shop Hours

Rather than an "open door policy," create a "closed door, open calendar" policy. Encourage others to schedule appointments with you at pre-determined hours of the day.

3. Set Voicemail Expectations

My voicemail lets others know that I will be checking my messages at noon and 4 pm. By managing the expectations of others, I allow myself to respond in a reasonable time frame.

4. Create a One-on-One Meeting Schedule

By setting a regular time and place to meet with your key contacts, you eliminate most interruptions. I've found that the majority of the "quick questions" discussed in the workplace can wait a few hours or even days.

5. Focus on the Person

When you switch task while working on a computer, you simply lose efficiency. But if you switch task on a human being, you damage a relationship. Be present, listen carefully, and make sure everything has been taken care of before moving on.

You Control Your Own Destiny

Essentially, you are your own boss because you work for yourself. As a result, you can be your best friend or your worst enemy. You control every aspect of your business, including the amount of time you put into your business. You can find yourself easily addicted to work, demands, and fulfilling all your professional duties. Deadlines and inventory checks might take precedence over a night with the girls, or that one soccer game. The trick is balancing work and play, and perhaps relaxing your own personal leash sometimes.

I find myself overwhelmed at times with a responsibility to achieve an incredible amount in my life. I'm not sure where it came from, although my family is definitely filled with dreamers and high achievers. I worry about the dogs that roam the streets, or are abused. I worry about my daughter and her friends, and how they will deal with the overwhelming issues that face them as young people in this crazy world. I worry about my family, my husband, and my good friends—wanting them all to be happy and fulfilled. I worry about my franchisees doing well and thriving in this time of economic uncertainty.

The problem isn't necessarily that I worry, per se, it's that my entrepreneurial "get-it-done" personality feeds a drive to *do* something about it. I can't just let sleeping dogs lie, I need to find them homes, darn it! All kidding aside, I recently decided to focus on a problem that I have the resources to help solve. I have over 200 franchisees and over 100,000 camp clients nationwide who can help me make sure that our furry canine friends are taken care of. Gandhi once said something to the effect that a culture is judged by how it treats its animals. So with all of the overwhelming responsibilities Americans face each day in trying to save the world (or at least the dog world that many of you reading this are a part of), I believe we can do it one dog at a time. It's simple. It's not expensive, and it's not time consuming. Find one dog one home, one day at a time.

Make an Appointment with . . . Yourself!

You know the saying, "Take care of yourself first so you can take care of others better"? So much easier said than done! When the pressing responsibilities are looming, the last thing you want to do is to think of yourself. But here is my advice: *Learn to say no!* You have to take the time to recharge your battery, even if that might mean letting someone down. You are only human.

Block off time for you, that no one is allowed to touch. There is *always* some pressing issue with work that needs to be addressed. I like to say, "It's doggy day camp, not brain surgery." But you have to be committed to setting those boundaries and sticking to them. It's *really* hard! Also, building a business that my family and friends work for, or are involved with, makes it easier to hang out with them more! Tori has always gone on business trips with me, attended grand openings, gone to franchisee meetings, etc., so she knows the business, likes the people, and genuinely wants to be around it. Same goes for my other family members who work the business with me. Although it certainly has its challenges, it does create an atmosphere of family and camaraderie.

- Take "brain breaks" about once an hour. For example, stand up, stretch, and take a few slow deep breaths. You and your overwhelmed noggin will thank you.
- Organize your tasks one at a time.
- Perk up your mind and spirit. Meditation, yoga, or solitaire, anyone?
- This is the hardest one: Turn off your Blackberry, phone, and homing device—anything that rings. While you are taking time out to unwind, you need full concentration on you. It will be OK to separate yourself from your devices for half an hour. Seriously, it will be.

Set Up Stress-Free Zones

- Exercise! Take care of yourself, or you will not be able to hold up.
- Entrust! You have the power to delegate, and you should do so whenever possible.
- Engulf! Surround yourself with great people
- Prioritize! Focus on one task at a time.

My office is homey, warm, and comfortable. Our number one rule is: Dogs are not only allowed, they are encouraged. It is a soothing, happy addition to our office that also serves as a reminder that what we do every day is positively affecting our furry best friends everywhere. We offer much more than a drop-off location for pets while people work. We take pride in the many reasons people trust Camp Bow Wow to care for their loved ones, and we are active philanthropists for organizations who also love animals. I make sure to keep this in perspective as often as possible. Don't get me wrong, when we have personnel, legal or other issues (like every business does), it is easy to get caught up in the bureaucracy. But that's just when I hug Tori, Jason and my dogs, take a deep breath, and get back to work. That's what it's about. The pack you're fenced in with makes all the difference in your survival.

Some visitors may think we have "gone to the dogs," but we feel that having our furry friends around during the weekdays alleviates stress, forces us to stop and "sniff the roses" a few times a day, and always brings a smile to the faces of visitors to our office. Typically, we've found that vendors that come in who do not feel comfortable in this atmosphere are probably not people we would do business with anyway!

I wish everyone could bring their furry friend to work with them like we do. What a better place corporate America would be!

How to Find Work/Life Balance as a Mom

Her cape is carefully tucked underneath her shirt as she flies through her days with the greatest of ease. Well . . .sort of. I am talking about the wonder women of the world—Moms in Business.

My mom and my grandmother were both strong women who instilled in me that I could do anything I wanted. They were strong believers in higher education, giving back to their community, and doing something they were passionate about. I retained from my mother the ability to believe I could be a great mom and still find time to help others. My mom raised me, and my younger brother Patrick, while forgoing paid work in favor of community volunteering efforts. She was very committed to launching the YMCA in our small community, and later when I was in college, devoted to opening a teen center. We were middle class and struggled financially, but my folks always found a way to make things happen for us and still give back to others. They were always thinking creatively, and not just about the community. They bought my best friend, who was struggling, a prom dress and taught her to drive because her mom was a single parent and was unable to do this herself.

Lessons Learned in Juggling

Starting and operating Camp Bow Wow is in many ways analogous to my life as a single parent. My experience as a single mom of both a daughter and a company that grew-up alongside one another provides various lessons in balancing work and life. Being a single mom has been the biggest challenge of starting a business, especially with all the traveling I have to do. Even though I am fortunate to separate business and the responsibility of being a mom, it gets difficult sometimes. There have definitely been some hardships and struggles from traveling that road alone. *Time, energy and resources* are three elements that have been absent, sometimes all at once.

It's so hard to be everything to everybody. I tried to be a great mom, a great boss, a great wife, a great daughter, a great friend, etc. It is exhausting. You are amazing, but you can't be all these roles all the time.

How did I balance being a mother and a businesswoman? Using a lot of the same principles—discipline, fun, variety, and commitment.

Lesson One: Admitting

Being successful in both worlds means knowing you can't do every little thing. Say it with me, "I can't be everything to everyone." Now that that's out of the way, we can tackle how to effectively provide for our children—and also inspire them!

Lesson Two: Pick Your Priorities

At some point, you just focus on the top priorities as best you can. For me, it's family, friends and business.

Lesson Three: Take Out the Trash

Get rid of people and projects in your life that squeeze too much out of you.

Lesson Four: Live in the Moment

You take one day at a time—one hour at a time and one minute at a time—and look to spend your time the most valuable way you can.

Lesson Five: Don't Expect Perfection

In a perfect world, I could sit down with Tori for breakfast, lunch, and dinner, get to every extra-curricular event, and, all the while, have a smoothly running franchise. That's not likely. Instead, I find a way to *make* time for Tori. I typically work in the morning for a few hours before I wake my daughter up. I stop working when I pick her up from school and start back for a few more hours after she goes to bed.

Lesson Six: Combine Schedules

I've had to work some crazy hours to fit it all in. I've had to do conference calls from ballet practice, bring Tori to business meetings, etc. Make sure you bring your child to work, not the other way around.

Lesson Seven: Sacrifice

I know it's hard, but you have to give up important meetings or tasks to put your child's needs first. I constantly try and put Tori first, like missing a franchise conference because her swim meet regionals were that weekend.

Lesson Eight: Ask for Help!

What to do when you have forty dogs you are caring for, and your daughter's school calls to tell you she is sick and needs to be picked up? Call on your close friends and family to help in a pinch! It may feel awkward at times, relying on others for help, but the hardest part is asking for it. Usually you'll find your loved ones are more than happy to help you out. My family and friends, and even my office manager, pitch in and help with my daughter. Without them, I wouldn't have been able to do this. Their wonderful support allows me to schedule my life around my daughter, even though I typically work ten to eleven hours a day.

In the end, I love my life—it's crazy busy and too much for a lot of people, but it is also filled with so much love, laughter, drama, challenges—it's very fulfilling.

CHAPTER 17

Best in Show . . . and in the Dog House

No matter what sector entrepreneurs advance in as the "Best in Show," they are typically presented with hardship and corresponding instability, but they find a way to overcome these trials without giving in to fears and doubts. One of the best examples is of a young woman in her mid-twenties who bought a struggling Camp Bow Wow and, with the help of family financing and the advice of other franchisees, turned the underperforming business into a popular camp with a tremendous surge in sales. She has since opened a second location, which quickly became another shining example of her devotion to working the plan and following the best practices created by the folks who came before.

At Camp Bow Wow, the Best in Show franchisees realize that they do not need to forge a new path, and that they can rely on successful business models created by fellow franchisees.

Nancy, our original Best in Show, bought our first franchise off of a sign on the lobby desk at the central Denver camp. God love her, she was a trooper. I already had a site in mind, an old foam manufacturing plant in the heart of Castle Rock, Colorado. Luckily, there was no zoning required and it was probably the only location in a twenty-mile radius that we could have hoped to get through zoning in Douglas County. However, the building was a complete and utter nightmare. Have you ever seen the movie *The Money Pit* with Tom Hanks? Well, it was the same property catastrophe, the landlord had done nothing to code, and it was a mess. The man avoided us like a perpetual plague, and because he lived in Wisconsin, it was especially easy to evade all of our calls and letters. The plumbing leaked, and the bicycle seats in the walls that he used to insulate were a fire hazard. Not to mention the heating unit didn't end up working. To get a permit for a new one, the place would have to pass an inspection. It definitely was not going to pass without a lot of work, so Nancy and I decided to roll up our sleeves and make it happen. My dad, Patrick, Nancy, her parents, her handyman, and even Tori, all worked diligently day and night to fix up the place. It was the dead of winter, and there was no electricity or gas hooked up, so we rented portable propane heaters to take the edge off the ten-degree winds blowing through the building. Challenging days like these exemplify the power of hard work and great people around you.

Nancy, using her sensational charm, befriended the city building department, and somehow we pulled off a miracle. We received the Certificate of Occupancy after two months of craziness, and she opened the day before Thanksgiving. A slew of potential franchisees poured in soon after with Wendy buying the second Camp Bow Wow we opened in Broomfield, Colorado. Tanya, Kevin, Aaron and Leslie took the leap with us by signing on for Colorado Springs and Fort Collins, Colorado, locations. April and Renee bought Central Denver as a franchise, and Bob and Ann became our first out-of-state franchisees in Troy, Michigan.

Let's take a look at some of Camp Bow Wow's top dogs and how they set the bar for being successful franchisees, or "zees."

Why Our Franchisees Do Well

They Are Honest

I stress a great deal the importance of honesty and that our franchisees understand and abide by this principle. Kennel cough is one of the many hurdles in running the camps and has been quite a challenge for many owners. At an annual meeting, two franchisees confessed that when they first opened, they found it difficult to be open with their customers about kennel cough because they were scared of the impact the sickness would have on their business. Over time, they learned that honesty is the best policy, and that the customers respected their integrity and stayed loyal to the business. They knew they could trust Camp Bow Wow to put the safety of their dogs first, no matter what unavoidable concern was at hand, especially money.

They Are Innovative

Truly Best in Show franchisees do not sit back and watch the business change. They change with the business! I have implemented a specific guideline for the franchisees, but I leave room for them to use their own creativity to expand on their camp. Our Best in Shows trust the value the franchise provides, but strive to better the system. Tony heads up the St. Clair Shores, Michigan, camp, and not only is a dog lover, but is also an extremely intuitive businessman. He is constantly developing cool incentives, such as a monthly membership program and charitable initiatives. Working with caused-based marketing has pushed him ahead in the game, and he receives a consistent five-star report among his customers.

Nancy runs our Chapel Hill, North Carolina, camp, and was recently invited to lead an open forum portion of our Camp Scout call. One of the key takeaways from her presentation was that her camp does a different marketing promotion every month of the year. Whether it's a charity fundraiser doggy wash, photos with Santa, or sponsoring community 5K races, her customers have come to expect the fun promotions and look forward to them each month She also mentioned that the promotions and events started out small and have grown over the years as her customers start to look forward to them, which is important for other young camps to recognize so they don't get discouraged while trying new promotions. Building a customer base is important, but building loyal clientele is even more rewarding.

Our Best in Shows are constantly seizing opportunities to work with others in the business. Carol from Cincinnati does just that by utilizing an exceptional and established dog trainer as a cross-seller. She doesn't charge her rent or tax her fees, and Carol believes it brings in a large additional revenue stream to her camp. This partnership is so affective that she's working to find an established groomer for the same reason.

They Are Dependable

The obvious front-runners are those that step up during disasters. You show your true colors when your back is against the wall. Let me tell you, our franchisees are no strangers to the unexpected! They have gone through floods, fires, windstorms, tornadoes and vehicles crashing into the building. I think that someone has even dealt with a city locust infestation during one of our trainings! This covers almost all of the biblical plagues, and then some.

The little things that seem so minuscule are the keys to being a dedicated business owner. These include such things as sitting in a vet's office with a customer late into the night just to make sure they have emotional support. Or rushing to your camp at inopportune times just to make sure your boarders are safe if you happen to see a tornado warning. Or *never* missing phone calls to the front desk, no matter what. The phone is answered, even if you have to ask a customer to hold. If it goes to voicemail, you might as well assume that they have already called your competitor.

They Have a "Pawsitive" Attitude

An uplifting and affirmative attitude is essential to any thriving franchise. Anyone willing to help others in the system will quickly become Best in Show. It's smart to take the time to get out in your community to be a true community member. For the South Windsor, Connecticut, camp, Tami has the attitude and assertiveness to be successful. Like many of our franchisees, she's a self-starter and entrepreneur, but unlike some who say they can do it and don't, she really follows through with what she's doing. She has a lot of connections in the community, and because she has an outgoing personality, people give her camp a lot of support.

This kind of word-of-mouth advertising makes up a huge part of our business. After some heavy convincing, Tami did hire a Camp Scout, and has gotten very good at delegating some of the marketing work, which at first, like many others, she insisted on doing herself. I'm sure if you asked her directly, she would tell you the franchisee can't do it all themselves, no matter how good they are, and that it's imperative we all work with each other to help grow the business.

A negative attitude does not attract new customers. If a franchise owner has a negative outlook on life, the business, and everything it encounters, the customer will pick up the negative energy when they walk in the door. If a customer feels this way, do you think they will come back? Not likely.

They Understand the Importance of Customer Service

Our Best in Shows concentrate on exceptional and unparalleled customer treatment. For their customers, each visit feels like the first time, and they leave feeling genuinely taken care of with exceptional follow-up. The most inexpensive, but highly effective, way to market is by merely *thanking* your customers for their business and *asking* them for more.

Listen to what the customer wants and then deliver. There is nothing worse than losing a client to something as simple as attention to detail. A customer feels very betrayed when they specifically ask for something a certain way and do not receive it. Communication is key; take notes and follow up with your internal team. During these meetings, put yourself in the place of the customer and what you might want to see. That might mean hiring a full-time front desk receptionist, or dedicating someone to the maintenance of your online community networks. Two heads are better than one; three heads are better than two, and so on. When you work with your team for the benefit of the customer, you cannot fail.

Worst in Show: Why do Franchisees Fail?

A lot of people come into this business thinking how fun it's going to be to hang out with dogs all day. But we are taking care of people's furry children, all day and night, 365 days a year! It is an all-consuming business and you have to know so much more than people think—everything from dog behavior to disease management, in addition to the nuts and bolts of running a business. We get franchisees from so many different backgrounds, and they all have a love of dogs in common, but we have to teach them to be businesspeople, and to market the business and not just focus on the dogs. It's a challenge to find people who want to make it a real moneymaker and not just a labor of love.

Reasons Why Franchisees Are Not Successful
They're the Lamb, Not the Lion

Lack of intestinal fortitude is the culprit that causes many franchisees to sink. When the going gets tough, many cannot find the nerve to stick it out. As an entrepreneur, you have innate qualities that set you apart from the average worker. But what you really need is *courage* to last as a business owner. In order to make a success out of something, you need to understand the tough world we live in is unforgiving and ever-changing. It's easy to have the head for business, but without the guts, you cannot become the leader of the pack.

Expensive Start-Up

At Camp Bow Wow, one key mistake is underestimating the extent of construction or development needed for the purchased camp. Franchisees fail to look at the money they spend on their camp as an investment versus a payout scenario. They get in over their head from day one, and it's harder to progress past the first year.

One franchisee chose not to use our construction management team. He didn't adhere to the standards and specifications set by the franchise, and he ended up performing part of the construction himself. By not hiring professionals, his attempt at being cost effective proved to be counterproductive in terms of time and money. The professionals had to work around him, thus taking more time and effort and charging more. He could have been open six months prior to his opening date. In franchising, the key is learning from those that went before you—follow the system and avoid mistakes that others have made!

Their MO Is Morally Off

If you come into this business with a slanted method of working, you are setting yourself up for failure. Some franchisees believe their way is the best way, and this goes against the function of a franchise. The incentive to purchase, besides the brand, is to take advantage of the large networking system you instantly inherit. When you believe your way is the best, you choose not to interact with fellow franchisees and the franchisor, and thus miss out on time-tested practices that work. These franchisees haven't fully bought into the tried-and-true program, and try to cut corners while going at it on their own. They do not take advantage of the benefits the franchise offers, such as:

- Help from corporate
- Help from other franchisees
- Participation in proven programs

Instead of delegating, they think they can do it all, which is downright impossible.

On the flip side, some franchisees believe the franchisor should do all of the work for them, and they take no initiative whatsoever with having any business sense. They blame others for their failures, instead of doing something about it. Many of them do not have the outgoing personalities to gain the support of their customers and communities. So, although they may get people in the door once or twice, they have not spent enough time building customer loyalty and retention, and their customers have no reason to come back. Also, because of their harsh or quiet personalities, they haven't been able to hire great staff, so they are hurt twice (once for not representing their company well to the public, and twice for not having the right staff to do it for them).

Luckily, at Camp Bow Wow, we have a tremendous group of franchisees who have helped us build an incredible brand. The few who have faltered have left the system on their own, or have delegated the running of their operations to a manager who has the devotion and savvy to run a great camp.

CHAPTER 18

Growing Your Business

Putting in the extra effort with your company places every business owner in the top dog category. With limited financial help available, small cash-strapped businesses must think of creative ways to push their business forward.

Word of Mouth

Where you can spark interest? Center on those resources to get hits. The Internet, radio, and TV are all great mediums for publicity, but don't forget about human relations and word of mouth.

PR is a necessary way to get word out about the business. It's really just about telling your story in an interesting, effective way. We receive a lot of leads on possible new franchisees through word-of-mouth from our existing franchisees and open camps. This is one of the oldest marketing techniques, but it is still very effective. I tell people that we take one dog at a time, giving them the best care possible. When you pay homage to what your business stands for, the public follows suit with the concept and the company. PR was a huge catalyst for growing our brand, and it didn't cost us a thing!

Get Creative

Even when I was at the stage of opening my first camp, I would go out of my way to advertise. The first site was located in an old war veterans hall in downtown Denver. My brother ran the day-to-day operations, and I stayed out marketing like crazy, while working a full-time pharmaceutical job and juggling time with Tori. I initially enticed our upscale clients by going to dog parks with buckets of milk bones and starting up conversations about my business. I also used my pharmaceutical sales background to learn to network with area veterinarians for referrals.

Think Free

Non-profit work is another great way to get referrals. When you freely give up services, you are not only helping a worthy cause, but word will travel fast about your company lending a helping paw.

Publicize

Be kind to everyone and always accept an interview; they are a great way to get free publicity. We have been featured on AOL's main page, Donny Deutsch's *The Big Idea*, the *Wall Street Journal*, CNN, *Success* magazine, and other great media outlets. Since our dog camps focus on a safe place for traveling parents, we also advertise in the airline magazines.

Taking Advantage of the Digital Age

We are living in a technology-driven age, and businesses that add the support of innovation and mechanics will see positive results. People love convenience and accessibility, two traits that you should always cater to. My experimental web cam addition has grown to be one of the most beneficial assets to Camp Bow Wow. When formulating the idea, I wanted to give my clients a level of support and comfort. So whether your pooch is prancing in the Puppy Pasture, or cuddling around the Campfire Circle, you can watch your pal with ease. Each area at camp is wired with a live streaming web cam that you can watch from our website. On the website you have the ability to zoom-in or zoom-out on any of the eight cameras and even take a picture with the freeze-frame snapshot function.

I am constantly hearing appreciation for this tool from dog owners, saying it gives them a peace of mind while they are either at work or on vacation. When they miss their pup, they can log in and see a live-stream video. We now have a Rover Cam that attaches to the dog's collar, and our new mobile doggy cam technology allows you to view it on your cell, too!

The Internet is a wonderful resource that should not go untapped. We utilize our website as a marketing tool by listing our story, service description, camp location, and featured articles. Social networking is a major trend that has been growing significantly with the online community. Small business should be involved with the larger social networks, such as a blog or forum. A community blog is a great way to reach and interact with potential and existing customers. By giving updates in a personal, conversational way, you will easily spark interest and allow clients to engage and grow with your company. You can post videos, start discussions, and respond to questions.

Whether you have a team of seven or 700, it's important to appoint someone with the responsibilities of maintaining the website and social networking. There are many ways to "bare-bones" network if small business owners cannot afford to hire outside help. MySpace, Facebook, LinkedIn, and Twitter are all social sites that small business owners should think about. These free sites allow members to network with each other and establish themselves in different groups. By giving your company an account, you can grow your exposure to the market and potential clients. Your friends in the community can refer you to their friends, and best of all, it doesn't cost a dime. Also, assure each site has a high Google page rank, so when your name is searched on Google, you will be at the head of the search results. Just make sure you establish your identity on these sites, so you can protect your name against similar companies or competitors. Google Alert is another great tool that you can sign up for. When someone blogs about your company, you are immediately alerted so you can contact that person for further communication.

Be Careful . . .

It is the paradox of the communication and information age. Technology connects us more than ever before, but those connections are more tattered, fractured and incomplete than what we are used to. Virtually everything you do can be uncovered quite easily. The term "Google" is listed in *The New Oxford*

American Dictionary as the search for the name of (someone) on the Internet to find out information about them: You meet someone, swap numbers, fix a date, then Google them through 1,346,966,000 web pages. *The Pittsburgh Post-Gazette* reported a poll stating that 23 percent of people routinely search the names of business associates or colleagues before meeting them. Surveillance is somewhat transparent and you need to represent yourself in the way you want others to perceive you.

How Cause-Based Marketing Can Help Grow Your Business

Cause-based marketing, a type of marketing involving the cooperative efforts of a "for profit" business and a nonprofit organization for mutual benefit, has been a key strategy behind some of our country's greatest brands—Microsoft, McDonald's, Patagonia, Ben and Jerry's, Camp Bow Wow. And it can be the force that pushes your own business to new heights! A recent study has found that U.S. corporations are strongly committed to cause-related marketing, with many businesses planning to increase funding for these types of programs.

I have always had a devotion to making sure we don't put the "dollar before the dog." I have always done my best to ask myself, "Is this the best thing to create a happy, healthy, safe experience for our campers?" That focus and commitment has kept us on track. It's that old adage, "Do what you love and the money will follow." I think our human clients sense that we truly care about their dogs and want the best for them.

Here are some additional research numbers about the power of cause marketing (from a Cone Corporate Citizenship survey):

- 89 percent of Americans believe corporations and nonprofits should work together to raise money and awareness for causes.
- 76 percent of Americans believe partnerships result in a more positive image for the nonprofit.
- 79 percent of Americans are more likely to buy a product that supports the nonprofit.
- 76 percent are more likely to tell a friend about the nonprofit.
- 70 percent are more likely to donate money to the nonprofit when corporate and nonprofit interests are working as one.

- 75 percent of Americans feel nonprofits would benefit from having employees of the partner company volunteer for the nonprofit.
- 66 percent would welcome information about a cause or charity on the company's product or packaging.

With these statistics, it's easy to see why working for the greater good is a wise business move. Cause marketing is a great way to build positive brand awareness, customer loyalty and employee pride. How do you include cause marketing? Four essential elements to consider:

1. Identify a cause that matters to your audience.
2. Make it matter to you.
3. Promote it everywhere.
4. Make cause marketing a passion.

Giving back and contributing to the betterment of society has always been paramount for me. I absolutely believe we can create a world where all dogs have a home, and we can stop overpopulation. We have to take one dog at a time and one issue at a time. It's been my goal since day one to do something I was passionate about and be able to make a difference in the lives of animals. In fact, it was the main reason I started the business. I wanted the camps to give back by fostering dogs, reaching out to our customers to donate to dog charities supporting education on canine cancer, canine health and overpopulation. We would donate money and time directly to all kinds of smaller organizations and causes.

We currently sponsor a Ph.D. fellow in canine cancer research at Colorado State University's veterinary school, and we are working toward funding organizations that go into poor areas in the U.S. and elsewhere to spay and neuter stray dogs. We undertook a rescue mission abroad after our in-house counsel vacationed in Greece, a country with no Humane Society, and saw how poorly strays were treated there. We brought twenty-six dogs back over the past year and fostered them until we found them homes. I can't think of a better feeling than seeing the dogs playing and having fun, especially the dogs we helped find a new life off the streets. I think of the 2,500-plus dogs we've found homes for across all camps, and it makes me even more determined to make a difference and grow the business!

Camp Bow Wow has always championed cause-based marketing efforts, urging my franchisees to give back to the community and to the dogs by fostering pets in need of homes and holding fundraisers for local rescue and canine causes. As an example, CeCe and Janet, our Northglenn, Colorado, franchisees, bought an existing camp that was underperforming. They focused on cause-based marketing and building their foster dog program right off the bat. They worked with local dog rescues and had great success spreading the word about their camp through these organizations. Their business is ramping well now and beginning to thrive, while they continue to find more and more dogs new homes in their market. What a win-win for the clients and the camp!

The Bow Wow Buddies Foundation

With my for-profit business a success, I brought that same passion for dogs to the nonprofit area by creating The Bow Wow Buddies Foundation in 2007.

The foundation has enriched my business beyond bottom-line profits, while also helping to build a brand of trust and authenticity. I found an incredibly rewarding way to honor my commitment to the well-being of my beloved animals and to give others a chance to share in that commitment.

BOW WOW BUDDIES: LENDING A PAW

Our Mission

The mission of the Bow Wow Buddies Foundation is to promote the health and welfare of dogs worldwide by focusing on finding foster and lifetime homes for unwanted dogs, promoting humane education and treatment, and investing in research and treatment for dogs devastated by illness and disease.

Current Initiatives

Homing: Every dog deserves a loving home. The Bow Wow Buddies Foundation works with Camp Bow Wow doggy day care and overnight camps throughout the country to provide foster care and facilitate adoptions for homeless pets. Since 2003, we have found homes for over 2,500 dogs—and we plan to find forever homes for an additional 2,000 dogs this year.

Health: Working to find a cure for canine cancer is our top priority. In addition to funding a yearly scholarship at the world-renowned CSU Animal Cancer Center, Bow Wow Buddies has launched "Lend a Paw for the Cure," a campaign to raise money and awareness for the research and treatment of canine cancer.

Humane: All dogs have the same basic needs— clean food and water, shelter and love. Worldwide dog overpopulation leads to neglect, abandonment, abuse and suffering. Recently, the foundation rescued twenty-six dogs from Greece, a country that has no large-scale animal welfare infrastructure, yet faces some of the most horrific and violent cases of abuse and neglect imaginable. We are also working on spay/neuter programs around the U.S., and supporting humane education on the horrors of puppy mills in our country, as well.

Considering Expanding Your Business?

If you focus on services instead of products, you might want to cross the line and tackle both. You need to be focused on your core business until it's proven you have it down. Once you conquer your core, *then* you can add on other revenue streams. Be wary of going too fast too soon, or you'll overwhelm your team and your customer. You have to earn the right to grow your brand.

I am a huge advocate for companies that are based on going against the grain. But when it comes to branching out, it's wise to follow the path of least resistance. Make sure the addition is in a market that is adjacent to what you are already doing. You will also have to do a lot of financial and personal analysis to figure out if you can make that leap. Plus, you need to make sure your team can handle the extra work—it's like starting a whole new business!

Whether new additions are foreseen or not, always keep your ears perked for a new project or opportunity. With each prospect comes the possibility of capitalizing.

I am always thinking of ways to cover other demographics with our brand. We are now grabbing a slice of the retail pie by offering such items such as dog backpacks, stuffed animals, and squeaky toys for sale at our camps. These products are all along the lines of our signature "mountain lodge" theme. Since my customers are all dog lovers, the retail line is an obvious choice. Just concentrate on what your clients might want or use and it may spark some great opportunities for you. And since you are already a known entity, you already have a foot in the door and can easily sell your new extension.

Presenting Home Buddies!

This year, I've started a sister brand to Camp Bow Wow called Home Buddies. It is an in-home pet care service (either with someone there overnight, or just checking in). Services include: dog walking from the home, poop scoop services, doggy adventures (groups of dogs are taken on field trips to the mountains, beach, dog park), pet shuttle service in our Bark-n-Ride van, and special needs care for animals after surgery, or who need meds. We also offer mobile dog/cat grooming and dog training. A big differentiator for us is our innovative in-home web cams to allow you to log in while you are gone and check in on your pets!

We've been contemplating entering the in-home pet care market for several years, but thought it was best to wait until we really had our core competencies down—day care and boarding. As the recession hit at the end of 2008, we decided our camps needed an additional revenue source in case the day care/ boarding business was affected. We also needed a less expensive franchise model to sell, as the SBA loans for our camps were getting more and more difficult to obtain, due to increased lending requirements.

Home Buddies is a natural complement to our business—many of our clients have older, younger, or less social dogs that aren't appropriate for our camps, and they also need care. They also have other animals—cats, rabbits, fish, and snakes—that need care as well! Several franchises were popping up that focused on one niche—pet sitting, mobile grooming, training, poop scoop services—so we thought we would create a "one-stop shop" franchise that people could call on. Not to mention that they already trust our brand and feel comfortable leaving their animals in our care.

Expanding Your Business through Franchising

Initially, I was happy to have four or five dog camps here in Colorado. One day, I was speaking to a camp client who was a regional field director for Mrs. Fields Cookies, and he asked me if I ever thought about franchising. The more I looked into it, the more I saw the fit. For me, franchising took the best parts of my personality. I got people excited about building a concept, and I could get more of these places up and running while growing a system.

Surprisingly, no one else had franchised in the dog boarding/dog care segment, so I saw it as a great opportunity. It also took advantage of my love of growing the brand. But my lack of enthusiasm over running the day-to-day camp operations, that would be the franchisees' role. Franchising is more about being a visionary and seeing the overall picture. I had great success in franchising, due to the mentors I had along the way. I found a wonderful source of information when I went to an International Franchise Association meeting and was able to connect with some great folks in the industry. They became paramount in helping me learn the franchise business.

I dove in without really knowing the horrific nightmare that franchising can be, and how ridiculously expensive it can be with legal issues, accounting rules, support systems, cash flow demands, and so on and so forth. Try out your business plan in one location first to make sure it works, and then try a second or even third location before you think about franchising. There are a lot of restrictions, and it's not the easiest way to grow your business. If I could do it all over again, I would have had more seed money, and I would have had a more formal franchise business plan. I just held on to my gut feeling that I was supposed to be growing Camp Bow Wow and make it happen. I was also lucky my first franchisees were so helpful!

Is Your Business "Franchisable"?

- It needs to be credible. Potential franchisees need to believe they are buying into a business that the public trusts and wants to partner with for services or products. Credibility is the key to franchising successfully.

You have to offer customers a proven service with valued systems and processes they can rely on every time they visit the business.

- It needs to be unique. There should be a value added to the opportunity—something they can't go out and start on their own easily and quickly. At Camp Bow Wow, our unique way of caring for the dogs by allowing them to play all day, and the availability of web cams to monitor them, is a unique offering that is difficult to replicate.

- It needs to be teachable. Franchising is about teaching others how to operate the business model effectively to grow the brand quicker than if you did it on your own with each store. Documented systems and procedures, and a solid business plan for start-up, is part of what folks are buying when they purchase a franchise.

- It needs to provide an adequate return. You've got to prove your business model before you franchise. If you can't make money with one store, chances are no one else will have a good shot at it either. Get your financial model set and successful before you recruit others to follow in your footsteps.

The Upside to Franchising Your Business

Franchisees provide:

- **Start up and operating cash:** If it costs several hundred thousand dollars to open one corporate unit, the rate of growth to do it on your own will be much slower than if you have ten people willing to franchise and put the money up to open the units. It then grows the brand exponentially, without a tremendous amount of start-up capital out of your own pocket.

- **Management of units:** Franchising allows you to tap into people who are much more committed to a successfully run business than a store manager you'd hire on your own. They have a lot invested into making it work, thus they are much more willing to do what it takes to see that the unit is profitable and that the customers are treated well.

- **Investment of time to open more units:** Our camps take an average of twelve months to open, so you can imagine how much longer it would have taken us to get to 100 units if we opened one or two at a time.

Franchising allows us to open twenty to thirty camps at a time, while quickly growing the brand.

Why Not Franchise Your Business? Downsides . . .

- **Quality control:** As your franchise company grows, it gets harder and harder to control what your franchisees do in the day-to-day operations and marketing of their business. Without being there every day with them, it's hard to track. It's imperative you start with a strong franchise agreement that allows you opportunities to enforce violations of the brand and protect your system. Having field personnel and a tight operations manual will help keep your franchises running the way you want them to.

- **Franchisee business expertise:** It's a challenge to find folks that already have a lot of experience or expertise running a business. Therefore, a lot of your time as a franchisor will be spent coaching them and building systems to support their lack of knowledge in certain areas. We have a lot of passionate dog lovers who join our system, but many have never run a business. They struggle trying to combine their passion with the challenges that come with starting and operating their own business.

- **Managing the brand:** Your brand is your baby—you've got to hold up your vision for the brand, and wrap your high standards around it. Simple things like making sure the logo is correct, phrases are trademarked, web sites are standardized, and stores look alike—are all paramount in protecting your brand as it grows. Consistency is king!

- **High-maintenance franchisees:** While *your* focus is on protecting and growing the brand, your franchisees' focus is on being profitable and running the day-to-day of their business. Some franchisees are very independent and don't want a lot of support, while others call non-stop! The systems and processes you develop for your franchisees to use will be critical in supporting them, so you don't always have to. The simpler you make it to run the business, the less they need from you on a daily basis!

What Are the Traits of a Successful Franchise Company?

1. *Your Brand* Is *Your Business*

Focus all business decisions on building and protecting your brand, including selecting a URL, name, and a logo that can be trademarked nationally. In the end, the intellectual property is what franchisees are buying for their franchise fee and ongoing royalties.

2. *Prove the Model*

Open one location to make sure it's profitable and easy to duplicate before you consider franchising. Folks buying a franchise from you will want to know that the model is proven to work, even if it's only at one or two locations.

3. *Cash* Is *King*

Make sure you have access to plenty of it to start and continue to operate your business. The number one reason small businesses fail in this country is because they run out of cash. The ability to use lines of credit, home equity, credit cards, or family and friends as back-up will be critical if you hit a bump in the growth of your business.

4. *Surround Yourself with Success*

Surround yourself with experienced, successful mentors and a great team. Interview the heck out of people and check all references—whether it's a consultant, a new hire, or a mentor. Make sure you start slowly with a short leash and make them prove themselves before they earn a longer leash with more leeway.

5. *Lay a Solid Legal Foundation*

Spend the time and money to hire the best legal counsel to create your franchise disclosure document and franchise agreement. These will be the basis of everything you do. The International Franchise Association (IFA) is a great place to start for referrals. Or talk with other small franchisors in your area.

6. Harness the Power of Technology

From your intranet to POS software, search engine optimization, and your corporate web site, technology will help you manage your growth and support the franchisees. It's a critical tool to use when running your business.

7. Find Balance and Boundaries

Happy franchisees make for a healthy franchise system! Keep them happy, but don't be afraid to set boundaries and protect the brand. It's a fine line to walk sometimes. Your franchisees are not always going to like you, and you'll certainly disagree at times. If you act professionally, focus the outcome on the overall good of the system, and don't tolerate any violations, you'll earn their respect and make it easier in the long run to have a good solid relationship with your franchisees.

8. Flexibility Is Vital to Your Survival

Adapting to a constantly changing market and business is critical. The business environment is changing every day; it's important to network and stay educated on business issues that will impact your company and your franchisees. It's more important than ever to be flexible when issues come up to keep the business growing and adapting to the rapidly changing market.

9. You Can't Manage What You Don't Measure

If you don't use metrics to measure the success of your business, you'll be relying on subjective data for your decision-making. Numbers don't lie, and they take a lot of interpretation and guess work out of decision-making around your business. It's easy to assume something is so, but without data you can measure, there's no back-up to make sure you are doing the right thing. It's great fun to watch your metrics grow and change positively—and if they are negative, it's urgent to see trends before they tank your business.

10. Find a Brand You Are Passionate About

I've said it before and I'll say it again: If you have passion in your job, you will not work a day in your life! Since you'll be working long hours and spending the majority of your resources on your new business, pick something you love! It makes it more fun and tolerable when you have to sacrifice in other areas of your life.

CHAPTER 19

Focus on the Ball

We all know the popular saying, "What doesn't kill you makes you stronger." For me, this statement is my own personal mantra. I have had so many barricades thrown in my path, that each one felt like it would bring me down in a ball of flames at some point. Some of my hardships have kicked me down so hard, it seemed impossible to get back up when I was in the throes of it.

After a year into the first camp, I quit my job in pharmaceuticals and focused my energy on turning the camp into something really special. I decided to expand my camp and open a second location a year after opening the first one. The second location was located in Broomfield, Colorado, a town close to Boulder.

Soon after, came the moment in my life that was one of the strongest tests to my endurance and perseverance in growing the business. I remember sitting alone on the floor of our second camp in the wee hours of the night laying tile. It was the eve of our grand opening that had been largely advertised throughout Colorado. Back then, it was tradition to pull an all-nighter before a grand opening, to make sure everything was tied up for when the masses showed hours later. I collapsed on the hard cool floor and realized I had rolled the dice with every penny to my name and was maxed out on credit cards, family loans and lawyer bills from my custody battle.

There was absolutely no money left anywhere, and my first rent check was due the next day. I was opening the doors to a second camp and I wasn't even making money on my first.

Oddly enough, I wasn't worried. I kept holding on to my dream and trusting that it would all sort itself out. Camp Bow Wow Broomfield made it, and I ramped it up fast. I spent twelve hours a day visiting vets, going to local businesses, attending networking events, hanging out at the dog parks—doing everything I could to get some money in the door to pay those first months' bills. Sheer tenacity and perseverance were the essential steps in making the subsequent camps happen. I held steady to a "Let's figure it out and move on" attitude. With a clear vision in my mind about what I wanted it to be, I didn't dwell on mistakes or missteps.

Camp Bow Wow is what it is today because I stuck with it. Don't abandon your baby at the first sign of trouble, or even the second! Or the third!

There are going to be numerous times when all you want to do is throw in the towel and give up. The problems keep piling up, and the light at the end of the tunnel seems to fade with each day. You think to yourself, "I did not see myself in this place six months ago! Where is the reward? Why are all these problems happening to *me*?" There is simply no success without hardship, so put on those fighting gloves and get back into the ring.

Use Mistakes to Your Advantage

Do not be afraid of complications related to starting your business. They mean you are stretching your limits and taking risks. Ultimately, that's what it takes to make a company successful. Look at your difficulties as puzzles that need to be solved on the road to success. With each lesson, you become more confident in the big picture, more focused on your vision and how to build it to the grandiose scale you know it can become. I can attest to a world of difference between my first and second camps due to my ability to learn from my mistakes. The second camp opening went so much smoother, and I knew what did and didn't work when marketing and dealing with customers. The business model was already there, and I had fun refining it with the second camp.

It's Not Personal

Try not to take things too personally and keep an open mind when analyzing why something didn't work. If you don't understand how history played out, it will repeat itself. Just detaching yourself emotionally from the failure helps a lot.

Step back and look at the situation as an outsider would. Ask others for help in reviewing the issue if you can't get there on your own.

Stay in the Game

I love the story of the high school basketball coach who was attempting to motivate his players to persevere through a difficult season. Halfway through the season, he stood before the team and said, "Did Michael Jordan ever quit?"

The team responded, "*No!*"

He yelled, "What about the Wright Brothers? Did they ever give up?"

"*No!*" the team resounded.

"Did Bear Bryant, the great college football coach ever quit?"

"*No!*" They yelled again.

"Did Elmer McAllister ever quit?" There was a long silence.

Finally, one player was bold enough to ask, "Who's Elmer McAllister? We never heard of him."

The coach snapped back, "Of course, you never heard of him—he quit!"

Accept Change

In our culture, we often relate change to a crisis, but I believe this is a misconception. Change equals opportunity!

You see, it's not what happens to us in life; it's what we do about it that is the true meaning of success. How we fail, how we deal with pain, and how we recover says much about the character of our achievements. My life has been filled with constant reminders of this truth. You need to be able to move with the changing times. Change is inevitable, so if you're ready for it, the shock will be less rattling.

Focus on What's Important

I center on the big picture when times get rough. I say, "Heidi, you're helping dogs, helping customers feel less guilty about leaving their dogs, and helping yourself, your staff and your franchisees live a fuller life." Even though Bion is gone, his spirit still lives within me as inspiration and guidance. He had absolutely no concept of fear. So when things are difficult, I say, "Move on." When the days seem endless and you want to tear your hair out, find ways to keep positive and elevate your mood. Surround yourself with supportive, uplifting people, or read motivational books and articles. Or, get out that old box of love notes, letters, or goofy pictures of you and your friends. During frazzled times when I feel beaten, I love to hear stories from my customers about how happy Camp Bow Wow made their dogs and them. I live in the *now* just like our furry friends!

To those who feel discouraged in the depths of pursuing their venture, it's worth the challenges and the wait. If starting a business were easy, then everyone would do it. And if running a successful business were easy, everyone would have one. Just remember that every dog has its day.

Unforeseen Complications

You have to expect the unexpected. My first bout of canine cough with some campers just about closed down the business. When I opened the business, I didn't know much about canine cough—only that we required a vaccination for it to come to camp and that would keep it away. Wrong! The vaccination only covers 40 percent of the strains that cause the illness, so dogs could still come down with it—and turns out they do fairly often. Our first bout caught us off guard and we ended up trying to pay for all the vet bills of the dogs involved in the outbreak. After digging into it and speaking with local vets, we started educating our clients about the disease, and told them to expect it at some point in their ongoing stays at the camp. Once we did that and set expectations with the clients, it was much more manageable to deal with when it happened again. People knew what to expect; they didn't freak out or expect us to pay for the vet bills. They knew we did everything we could to keep it away and protect the dogs. In a nutshell, canine cough is the equivalent of taking your child to day care and having them come down with a cold.

Lesson learned? Formulate plans to prevent reoccurring complications. I did not know what canine cough was and that it could put a pet daycare out of business. I had to research and learn about disease management, then I educated my staff and my customers on prevention and treatment.

When a dog gets hurt at camp (which is rare, thank goodness) I teach my franchisees what I learned—communicate how sorry you are for any part you or your staff could have played in the situation, tell them you will learn from it and do your best not to let it happen again, and ask, "What can I do to make it better?"

Another unexpected situation arose when a 160-pound Malamute surprised me on Christmas night the first year I had my second camp open. I stopped by around 11 pm to give the campers a special good-night treat. There were about thirty campers there, so I rotated the pups out into the play yards to give them a break before going to sleep that night. I let one particular group of large, rowdy Labs out and they immediately ran outside to romp and sniff. In the meantime, I let a big Malamute out of its cabin to stretch its legs, and as I was walking it toward the other play yard, it made a bolt for the door where the group I had just let out were playing. It literally dragged me to the door and shoved me through it to get to the other dogs (the door was left a bit ajar when I had put the other pups out).

As soon as I felt the air, I saw the other dogs rush the door to meet this new entry to the group. I was still holding on to the dog for dear life and hoping to pull him back through the door. No such luck. He lunged after the group and became very aggressive. The pack of Labs and the Malamute got into it, and I suddenly found myself in the middle of a full-on dogfight. I reached back to the door to get the hose that was just inside to break up the fight, but suddenly realized that the door had locked behind me. I was locked outside with the dogs fighting. An outside entry gate was my only means of escape, but I could not leave the dogs, so I was stuck. Two of the Labs cornered the Malamute and gave me enough time to push the Malamute down and lay on top of him to try to calm him. It took all of my weight and strength to keep him down. I searched my pockets for my cell phone and realized it had been thrown across the yard when I was trying to break up the fight. I couldn't move, or the dogs would be back at it, so I yelled as loud as I could for help. The condos behind the camp were dark, but I couldn't think of anything else to do.

With the commotion of me yelling, the Malamute pushed up and lunged for my neck. The two Labs immediately went after him to protect me, and one Lab was bit on the ear. I found my way back to lying on top of the Malamute when I heard someone climbing the fence to help me. The helpful neighbor went around to open the front door and let the dogs back inside while I stayed with the Malamute and kept him at bay. I managed to direct the dog into my car. Soon, animal control and the police showed up to help. The father of the dog's owner came and got him soon after, and I spent the next few hours at the emergency vet clinic with Duke the Lab, who lost a chunk of his ear trying to save me. Obviously, the Malamute didn't come back to camp, but Duke comes all the time—even now, six years later, as I gave him lifetime free boarding for helping me out.

Based on this incident, I implemented new policies concerning what dogs we would and would not accept, and I looked closer at procedures that would protect my staff better. I implemented a rule that no one can be at camp alone, unless all dogs are in their cabins. So ultimately, some good came out of the situation.

Staying Strong in the Dog Days of the Economy

I believe that relevant and essential brands will survive the current dog days of the economy. Experienced franchisors and entrepreneurs know that well-run businesses selling needed goods and services (with consistency and a smile!) can prosper even with dire macro-economic trends pitted against them. People still need haircuts, their morning coffee, vehicle repairs, and their lawns mowed. Tighten the belt, hold on to every penny, but gain market share where you can. The competition will be falling around you, so work hard to capture their customer base! Be creative in your approach to customers, showing them value when you can.

Many people have pegged the pet sector recession-resistant, myself included. It stood up to economic shocks in the year following 9/11, and again in 2005 after Hurricane Katrina. Each year is another test of that theory. Pet owners will continue to spend money on their companions in tough times, specifically on their care. Our customers are loyal and still need to travel—they just won't compromise their dog's care to save a few bucks. The latest available data from the Department of Labor shows that spending on pet services and veterinary services grew in the first two quarters of 2009 while the rest of the pet segment—products and supplies—slowed by 20 percent. So folks may cut back on the expensive collars and treats, but *not* on the high standard of care they have come to expect for their furry friends.

Even though our sector has held its ground, Camp Bow Wow and friends are still ultimately affected by this economy. New franchisees can't get their SBA loans through, and although we've tried everything, the funds are frozen due to the recent banking meltdown. We've had to get very creative with the way we open and finance camps to accommodate the new lending environment.

This is why we launched Home Buddies, a much less expensive franchise to start so folks can get financed and still live their dream of hanging out with animals all day!

There are certain uncontrollable circumstances where an entrepreneur cannot help but feel compromised, though. Figuring out how to work around what you can't control calls for putting a little spice on the grill. We brainstormed like crazy on other ways to bring in revenue with our brand without just selling franchises like we had in the past. We are now generating revenue off of our web site, through our in-house real estate and construction departments, with a new retail line of products, and with co-branding possibilities.

How to Recession-Proof Your Business

It isn't easy. I remember the weeks after 9/11. We all faced a huge unknown about the fate of our nation and our economy. We worked with our customers and fellow dog devotees to be creative and come up with ways they could continue to bring their dogs to camp, even without the security of a great job or a strong economy.

It's Always about the Customer

There is no more important time than now to be close to your customer and their attitudes and needs, and no better time to create trust and make your brand or company an easy, reasonable choice. Finding new customers through increased marketing and spending will be just as important as "wowing" your current customers through operational excellence. Offering over-the-top customer service, and following through on customer commitments, will give you the competitive edge to make it through a downturn. Our clients know our camps as Camp Bow Wow, not Heidi's Camp Bow Wow, or Katie's Camp Bow Wow. They expect the same level of care and support from every camp in the system. Consistency permeates great franchise brands and businesses, and it couldn't be more important than it is now!

A survey in 2008 was done of 10,000 sophisticated buyers. The question was, "What is it you buy when you buy? The company? The product/service? Or the person you deal with?"

What do you think was the overwhelming response? It's about the person! The relationship! 86 percent said *the* most important reason they buy is the person they're dealing with. This is the competitive advantage all of us are looking for in these rough times. It's so simple—build better relationships with everyone your business touches. This includes your clients, friends of your clients, the businesses in your neighborhood, etc.

The Department of Labor did a study of 6,000 buyers in 2007. The survey asked, "Why do you NOT do business with an organization?" Two-thirds said it had *nothing* to do with price. Two-thirds said it had *nothing* to do with quality of products or services. It has to do with *people*, with you and with your staff. If the communication breaks down, they'll stop doing business with you—it's that simple.

We are in the people business. People buy from people, people work for people, people quit on people, people fall in love with people, people get mad at people. Make sure your people are the reason you are keeping your customers in this downturn, not the reason you are losing them. Make your business relevant and essential to your customer.

Once a great and meaningful service is provided to a consumer, it is really hard for that consumer to give up that great and meaningful service. Yes, consumers will tighten their belts, and back off from some extravagant spending. But when it comes to time-saving products and services, such as Camp Bow Wow, which is so critical to their furry friend's care, you will be hard-pressed to find folks willing to give it up. The numbers mentioned earlier back that up; pet owners are cutting back on expensive products and supplies, *not* services. Make your services essential by taking the customer relationship to a whole new level. At Camp Bow Wow, we're revolutionary, but we're also a better value—hands down. Businesses that provide better value for their customers are more profitable during economic downturns and they grow faster after recovery.

Help Your Fellow Pup

Supporting the businesses around you boosts morale and camaraderie in your business community. As you work more closely with other businesses in your local market, your business will be more visible for less money, and you will all come out of the recession with greater momentum. Share becomes more important in tough times, and benefits go to those with resources to outspend the competition, integrate innovate new revenue streams and work smarter, not harder. When everyone is losing, the strong have an opportunity to become even stronger.

When I visit various markets and franchisees, I have started to see the incredible power of a market working together. The Southern California franchisees help each other with grassroots marketing, attending events, brainstorming ideas, and surviving tough times like the San Diego fires. Terri had snakes, birds, and cats all over her camp—and lots of support from her Camp Bow Wow friends. The Detroit franchisees put on a fantastic Texas Hold'em tournament to raise money for the Detroit Humane Society, and they have banded together to sponsor the group at a very high level! The New Jersey camps share ideas, customers and marketing efforts. Finally, the Denver franchisees rallied around Mutts and Models—a celebrity fashion show that brought awareness about their local camps to the whole metro area.

Spend!

Those who increase spending in economic downturns generally improve their market share, and therefore their profit. Those who increase spending significantly may have to absorb a short-term drop in return on investment, but they can then substantially gain share and greatly improve their position, and profit, for the future.

Spend "Found Time" on New Adventures

Slower business cycles allow you to attend to the ideas, professional development, and business-maintenance that you always wished you had time for. Use this time to reconnect with your vision, to develop specific areas of your business, to improve on what you're already doing well, etc. Build these activities into your weekly rhythm, ensuring that they remain when your enterprise is flush with business again. How about updating your web site more often? Kudos to those who take a negative and turn it into a chance to change, modify, and innovate.

Tap into History

Revisit successful approaches from the past. Reflect on the approaches that have worked well in the past, and that suit your vision, to earn new business. This thought-technique also strengthens your self-confidence, allowing you to see that you've successfully weathered storms in the past, and will do so again. After 9/11, we created special packages, fun events, and promos at the camps and worked even harder to build relationships with our customers. I think it was one of the reasons we are all still sitting here—it made us get creative and shift into the "out of the box" thinking that still permeates Camp Bow Wow.

Keep a Positive Outlook

Yes, the things we are doing now to address the economy were not necessarily part of my original plans. But I take a positive approach. It's diversifying our business and making us more sustainable. We wouldn't have been forced to explore these ideas without the economic downturn and banking crisis. My vision for the brand is staying in tact and the business is actually accelerating and expanding!

It's hard to deny we're in an economic downturn. But during this time, the world won't stop spinning and consumers won't stop spending. As our franchisee Kimberly Simons told me recently, "I refuse to participate in this economic downturn." I love it! It's the power of attraction and positive thought, the power for us to see this time as an opportunity for us to gain market share, sharpen our business skills and grow our brand more effectively!

Stress is an inevitable outcropping of economic downturns. Stress is *also* the foreshadowing of innovative breakthroughs and tremendous ideas. Channel any tension you might be experiencing into brainstorming sessions or solution-based thinking. These activities and their resulting actions also help to reduce stress. Start with the question, "If we don't want this, then what do we want?" Identify it—then visualize it!

Visualize Success and Create the Reality!

I want you to take out a pen right now and jot down what your idea of success looks like. Just pick three things that, if they happen, you will feel as if your business is a huge success. Pick goals that can happen realistically by the end of this year. Then fold up those slips of paper, and put them in the envelopes in front of you and seal them up. Take them out at the end of the year and see if you kept up with your goals. Success means different things to different people, but we can't actualize it until we can identify it.

CHAPTER 20

Conclusion: Happy Tails with a Happy Ending

You get one life to live, just one. If you're lucky enough, you have supportive friends and family to inspire, and keep you stable. But know that everything you need in life already exists within yourself.

It's been a long, tough road for me. There is a saying that goes that glass that's been shattered reflects the light in a beautiful way that it cannot if the glass remains intact. I've had my dreams shattered many times, but it's been the "getting through it" that has created my resilience and my faith in myself. I found love again a couple of years ago, after many tough years and many wrong relationships. Jason and I met through my employee/good friend Rebecca, and we hit it off immediately. Our third date was a night at the World Series, where our chemistry took off, and we knew we'd be together always. Jason has brought a lightness back to my life that had been missing since Bion died. My daughter, Tori, is a young, beautiful teenager now, with tons of life and energy, and lots of ambition to be a successful actress or singer! I'm very proud of the person she's become after all the turmoil that she has lived through. Tori recently got a little sister after years of hounding me about it, Holland Rebecca, or "Hollie" as we call her, was born in late July.

My parents and brother have had to heal over the years, too, but they are doing well and living life to the fullest as well. We've all come through this journey together, and have a definite appreciation for how quickly happiness can vanish, so we cherish every day and every experience. My dear friends who have been with me along this wild ride are like family to me. I've lost many friends through experiences with the settlement, the business, and the high demands of trust and loyalty that I place on those around me. Those that surround me now will be with me for life.

Tori's father has now been sober for a couple of years and is making an effort to be a bigger part of Tori's life. His family and I get along fairly well now, and the past conflicts seem to be a thing of the past. Now that Tori is older, I've explained to her in more detail the circumstances around her birth and the custody battle, but have also continued to encourage her to build a relationship with her dad and his family.

The Camp Bow Wow brand continues to grow at a fast clip with over 100 camps open, 200 franchises awarded, and a brand new franchise being launched called Home Buddies. Home Buddies will allow us to expand our love of animals and offer services for birds, cats, lizards, bunnies—you name it! Our franchisees will offer the home pet care services as a supplement to their Camp Bow Wow facilities. Our goal is to reach 500 franchises awarded, 250 camps open, 250 Home Buddies operating, and $100 million in system sales by the end of 2012. I've made it this far without bringing in any investors or selling any portion of the company, which has been extremely challenging, but should prove fruitful when I take the company public in the coming years. I've got a fantastic team now that I trust inherently and respect tremendously. That's quite a feat after all the crazy experiences with consultants, friends, family, employees who embezzled, took advantage, broke rules, and headed our company down the wrong path. I still love waking up every day and taking on the next business challenge, even after eight years of drama, excruciating decisions and crazy long hours.

I've also been able to realize my dream of creating a nonprofit organization, The Bow Wow Buddies Foundation, which promotes the health of pups, ending overpopulation and the inhumane treatment of animals worldwide. I've traveled to Greece with several team members and managed to save the lives of twenty-six "Greekies," or stray Greek dogs, as we nicknamed them. We've raised over $100,000 for canine cancer research, and we've adopted out over 3,000 dogs through our camps in the last few years. Our plans are to tackle overpopulation around the world in the coming years, and help cure canine cancer on the way!

The lessons I've learned over the years fill this book, but keep in mind that the world is your field of tennis balls and pile of sticks to fetch if you just put your nose to the ground and go after them! Tragedy, loss and misfortune can all be used to learn the lessons you will need to get past your fear and become a great leader or entrepreneur. So let's play ball!

About the Author

Through personal and professional tragedies, beginning with the loss of her young husband to losing a million dollar insurance settlement, Heidi has faced extraordinary adversity. By turning her life-long passion for dogs into the nation's largest doggy day and overnight care franchise company, creating a related charitable foundation, and raising a wonderful daughter as a single mom, she has accomplished great success so far. Through these experiences, Heidi has gleaned personal wisdom and business acumen which she is eager to share with those who are searching for fulfillment or wishing to find strength to face life's personal and professional challenges.

With her first husband, Bion, Heidi began building a life full of happiness and with a limitless sense of hope for the future. Two highly-motivated energetic twenty somethings with entrepreneurial spirits and an abundant supply of energy, they conceived the idea of starting a doggy day and overnight care business born out of their love for dogs and the need for a market alternative to the bleak conditions of the traditional kennel environment. With this motive, Camp Bow Wow was born. The concept was totally novel and in many areas of the country remains so to this day - the philosophy is simple, Camp Bow Wow is a place where a dog can be a dog.

As a young couple from middle class families, Bion and Heidi lacked the resources to start the business, so the plan was shelved until the "future". Their future together did not come as an unfortunate accident caused Bion's untimely death at age 25, which had a paralyzing effect on Heidi. For years afterwards, she lost sight of all the hope that gave her the drive to make something of her life. All the energy and spirit she once had was channeled into a myriad of wrong directions.

Finally, in 2000, as a somewhat lost, single mom, Heidi was encouraged by her brother to finally start Camp Bow Wow. She pulled the dusty business plan off the shelf, rolled up her sleeves and jumped head-first into the most challenging undertaking of her life which has grown to be the one of the largest women-owned franchise and pet industry businesses, the largest doggy day care company in the world and a $30 million leader in the $47 billion United States pet sector. This bumpy road has presented her with all sorts of trials and tribulations, but the rewards, mostly non-financial, have been unparalleled.

The timing to start Camp Bow Wow was perfect. Heidi was ready to devote herself to a business she loved and felt she had no choice but to succeed...failure was not an option! After investing the last of her savings ($83,000 to be exact!) and a lot of sweat equity, she opened her first camp in December of 2000 near downtown Denver. In 2003 she started franchising the concept and by 2007 sold over 200 franchise businesses. Camp Bow Wow came to fruition because she believed in herself, overcame fears, and shunned naysayers. Heidi respects and admires everyone who overcomes personal hardship, follows their passion, and comes out on the other side shining with their version of great success. Her story aims to offer encouragement and incentive as well as advice on overcoming extraordinary personal suffering to an audience who may be fearful of taking chances, growing or leading a business, or of ultimately achieving their dream.

To learn more about Heidi's dog care business visit:
www.campbowwow.com

To learn more about having Heidi speak at an event visit:
www.heidi-inc.com

To learn more about Heidi's Bow Wow Buddies Foundation's commitment to
the health, humanity and rehoming of our furry friends please visit:
www.bowwowbuddies.com

Have a Dog Gone Great Day!